rspb
POCKET

GARDEN BIRDWATCH

DK

LONDON, NEW YORK,
MUNICH, MELBOURNE, DELHI

ORIGINAL EDITION
Editor Rebecca Warren
Designers Francis Wong, Sonia Barbate
DTP Designer Laragh Kedwell
Production Editor Luca Frassinetti
Production Controller Susanne Worsfold

REVISED EDITION
DK London
Senior Editor Peter Frances
Editor Lili Bryant
Project Art Editor Duncan Turner
Senior Producer Alice Sykes
Pre-production Producer Rachel Ng
Jacket Designer Mark Cavanagh
Jacket Editor Manisha Majithia
Jacket Design Development
Manager Sophia MTT
Managing Art Editor Michelle Baxter
Managing Editor Angeles Gavira Guerrero
Publisher Sarah Larter
Art Director Philip Ormerod
Associate Publishing Director Liz Wheeler
Publishing Director Jonathan Metcalf

DK Delhi
Designers Shreya Anand, Upasana Sharma
Senior Editor Vineetha Mokkil
Editor Himani Khatreja
DTP Designers Vishal Bhatia, Sachin Singh
Managing Editor Rohan Sinha
Deputy Managing Art Editor
Sudakshina Basu
Production Manager Pankaj Sharma
Pre-production Manager Balwant Singh

Bird profiles written by
Jonathan Elphick
and John Woodward

First published in 2007 by
Dorling Kindersley Limited
80 Strand, London WC2R 0RL

This revised edition published in 2014
Copyright © 2007, 2009, 2014
Dorling Kindersley Limited
A Penguin Company

2 4 6 8 10 9 7 5 3 1
001 – 196330 – Jan/2014

A CIP catalogue record for this book
is available from the British Library

ISBN 978 1 4093 4627 2

Printed and bound in China by
Leo Paper Products

Discover more at
www.dk.com

Contents

Introduction 4

About birds 8
Territory 10
Singing 12
Courtship 14
Nesting and rearing 16
Migration 20
Feeding 22
Spring 24
Summer 26
Autumn 28
Winter 30

Birds in your garden 32
The garden habitat 34
Shelter 36
Natural food 38
Types of food 42
Feeders 46
Siting feeders 50
Making food 52
Water 54
Nest boxes 56
Making nest boxes 58
Threats to garden birds 60
Small gardens 62
Urban gardens 64
Suburban gardens 66
Country gardens 68

How to identify 70
Anatomy 72
Plumage and markings 74
Size and shape 76
Beak and tail shape 78
Wing shape 80
Watching 82
Bird profiles 86
Bird Gallery 108

The Big Garden Birdwatch 114
Index 124
Acknowledgments 128

Introduction

Gardens are havens for a wide variety of fascinating birds. Any garden, irrespective of its shape, size, or location, can be made attractive to birds, and you may be surprised at how many species will actually visit. Follow the advice in this book and the birds you attract and identify will give you countless hours of enjoyment.

About garden birds

Garden birds include familiar residents such as Robins, Blackbirds, and House Sparrows, as well as summer visitors such as Swifts and House Martins, which fly to the UK from Africa to breed. There are also species that come to the UK for the winter season, including Redwings, Bramblings, and Fieldfares.

More birds than ever before are making use of gardens, resulting in a rise in the number of species classed as garden birds. Woodland birds such as Great Spotted Woodpeckers, Siskins, and Nuthatches have discovered how to make use of the feeders and food provided in gardens.

Garden birds are easier to observe than the more reserved birds of the countryside. If you get to know their daily routine, you'll be able to watch the myriad of changes that occur in the life of a bird. Take care of the birds in your garden by providing food, water, and shelter and you will be rewarded with an endless display of avian activity on your own doorstep.

Garden oasis
Providing a source of water will reward you with close-up views of birds bathing and drinking, such as this Woodpigeon.

Feeding station
Supply the right foods and Greenfinches and Blue Tits will become a permanent fixture in your garden. You may even attract species such as Tree Sparrows (upper two birds pictured).

Bird-garden benefits

Gardens provide a vital habitat for birds. Their value increases with the ongoing loss of the countryside to development. Super-efficient pesticides mean less food for birds, and the loss of hedgerows has deprived them of nesting sites.

Thoughtfully managed, bird-friendly gardens can go some way to compensate for this. Taking steps to help garden birds provides benefits for you as well.

Each season brings new birds and different behaviour to observe. Seeing birds take to a new feeder and watching them raise their young are among the many activities that may take place in your garden. With a little effort, you can make a real contribution to the wellbeing of our bird life.

The bird essentials

You can cater for birds in any garden, whether you live in the middle of a city or in the country-side. It doesn't matter if you have an established garden or whether you are starting from scratch. It is even possible to provide food and nesting sites for birds if you don't have a garden.

All you have to do is remember what birds need, and provide it for them on a regular basis. This is not difficult and does not need to be expensive or time consuming. You can either transform your garden into a wild bird haven, or keep it simple by sticking to the basics – the choice is yours. Birds need four essential things – a regular supply of food and water, a place to nest, and somewhere to roost at night. Provide one, or preferably all, of these things in your garden and birds will come. Each of these four elements will be looked at in more detail later in the book.

A caring community

If you care for the birds in your garden, you are part of a growing community of "bird gardeners". More than half a million of these take part in the RSPB's Big Garden Birdwatch every January by spending an hour counting the birds in their garden. The enormous amount of data collected by keen garden birdwatchers helps to monitor bird populations all over the country.

Woodland visitor
The Nuthatch (left) is a bird of mature woodland, but providing the right food could attract it into your garden.

Frequent sight
Greenfinches are a year-round sight in gardens, never failing to entertain with their bright colours and comical squabbling at birdfeeders.

Record keeping
Have a notebook handy, so that you can keep a count of the number of birds visiting your garden, record interesting behaviour, or even make sketches. You could even keep a garden bird diary to record events throughout the year.

Close-up view
A pair of binoculars will show your garden birds in even greater detail and provide close-up views of their behaviour.

94

Fieldfare
Turdus pilaris

A large, handsome thrush with a striking combination of plumage colours, the Fieldfare is usually identifiable by its blue-grey head and white underwing. It is a winter visitor to most of Europe, like the smaller Redwing, and the two often feed together in mixed flocks, stripping berries from fruiting trees and shrubs.

FEEDS ON farmland, bushy heaths, woods, orchards, and gardens in winter; breeds in woodland.

blue-grey head with black mask
black and yellow bill
white under-wings
dark brown back
orange-buff breast with heavy black spots
pale grey rump
tail bars
white flanks
coarse black chevrons on white flanks

VOICE Loud, chuckling *chak-chak-chak*, thin nasal *weeee*; song a rather unmusical mixture of squeaks, warbles, and whistles.
NESTING Cup of grass and twigs in bush or tree; 5–6 eggs; 1–2 broods; May–Jun.
FEEDING Mostly eats worms and insects on the ground; also fruit from trees and bushes.
SIMILAR SPECIES Mistle Thrush, Blackbird.

95

Song Thrush
Turdus philomelos

Small, pale, and neatly spotted below, the Song Thrush is a familiar bird with a wonderfully vibrant, varied, full-throated song. Well-known for its habit of smashing the shells of snails to extract their soft bodies, it also feeds many earthworms from their burrows. It is declining in many areas, particularly on farmland.

BREEDS AND feeds in broadleaved woodland, farmland with trees and hedges, parks and gardens with shrubs.

orange-buff underwings
pale running
plain often unspotted uppertparts
plain wings
"V"-shaped brown spots
dark spotted white belly
dark-spotted yellowish-buff flanks
pale pinkish legs and feet

VOICE Short, high stop, song exuberant repeated phrases of musical and harsh notes.
NESTING Grassy cup lined with mud in bush or tree; 3–5 eggs; 2–3 broods; Mar–Jul.
FEEDING Takes earthworms, snails, slugs, insects, berries, and fruit, mainly from ground.
SIMILAR SPECIES Mistle Thrush, Redwing, female Blackbird.

Mistle Thrush
Turdus viscivorus

Big, bold, and aggressive, the Mistle Thrush is the largest of the European thrushes. It has a tall, long-necked look compared to the Song Thrush, and often flies much higher when disturbed. Males often sing from the tops of tall trees in all weathers, and in winter single birds defend berry-laden trees against Fieldfares, Redwings, and other birds.

BREEDS ON farmland and moorland near forest, woodland clearings, orchards, and parks.

bold dark eye
slender neck
grey-brown back
pale outer coverts
white underwings
pale rump
bold black spots on creamy buff underside

whitish tail sides
pale head
pale spots

VOICE Loud, rattling chatter, *tsairrr-tairr-tairr-tairr*; song repeated wild, fluty phrases.
NESTING Large cup of twigs and grass high in tree; 3–5 eggs; 2 broods; Mar–Jun.
FEEDING Plucks on ground, taking seeds and invertebrates; also eats berries and fruit.
SIMILAR SPECIES Song Thrush, Fieldfare, female Blackbird.

Redwing
Turdus iliacus

A small, sociable thrush with a bold head pattern and well-defined streaks below, the Redwing is named for its distinctive rusty-red underwings and flanks. It is a winter visitor to much of Europe from the taiga forests of the far north, and typically forages in flocks for berries, often with Fieldfares. In hard winters, it often visits large gardens for food.

BREEDS ON farmland and moorland near forest, woodland clearings, orchards and parks.

dark cap
bold pale stripe over eye
reddish underwing
dark brown back
bold pale stripe under dark cheeks
dull rust-red flanks
short, square tail

On calm, clear autumn nights, migrant Redwings can often be heard flying overhead, calling to each other to stay in contact.

silvery white below, with dark streaks

VOICE Flight call thin, high *seeeih*, also *chuk, chittuk*; song variable repetition of short phrases and chuckling notes.
NESTING Cup of grass and twigs, in tree bush; 4–6 eggs; 2 broods; Apr–Jul.
FEEDING Worms, insects, and seeds taken in autumn.
SIMILAR SPECIES Song Thrush, Skylark.

Bird profiles
These detailed profiles illustrate 40 regular garden visitors. Each entry gives key information about the bird's characteristics and is illustrated by a photograph of the species in the wild.

About birds
Understanding bird behaviour will give you a greater appreciation of the fascinating lives they lead, from nest building and raising a brood to migration.

Territory

A bird's territory contains everything it needs to survive – food, water, and shelter. Some species, such as Robins and Blackbirds, occupy the same area throughout the year, but most birds have separate territories for the breeding and non-breeding seasons.

Establishing boundaries

Breeding territories must contain enough food for a bird and its mate, plus their young. Males prefer a choice of nesting sites, and need several song posts from which to proclaim the boundaries of their territory and advertise their availability for mating.

Breeding territories are large, and can incorporate several gardens. Some birds may only visit your garden periodically. This is because their territory comprises a network of gardens.

Outside of the breeding season, birds only need to find food for themselves, and can patrol a smaller area. Many species, such as finches, Starlings, and tits, flock together once their breeding season is over – providing added security from predators. Other birds, such as Robins, have a solitary non-breeding territory.

Choosing a home

Finding the ideal home requires a lot of time and effort for a bird, but it is time well spent. Many of the best territories will already be occupied. The challenge is to find one that is

Domestic dispute
There is a hierarchy among tits, but this Blue Tit is making a valiant effort to defend its territory against the larger, more dominant Great Tit.

vacant or make a bid to steal one. Many birds start to search for a breeding territory in late winter to give them ample time to find a mate. Males must choose well – those with the best territories will attract the most female attention.

Musical markers
The male Robin performs a lengthy, varied song to mark the boundaries of its territory.

Non-breeding territories may be selected as early as late summer, when garden birds, including juvenile birds, venture away from their breeding sites.

Territorial defence

Fighting is a common sight during the breeding season. If warning signs such as aggressive posturing and singing fail to deter intruders, territory-holding birds may be forced to get physical.

Chases may end with the birds coming to blows, but don't be concerned if you witness this – it is natural behaviour and the birds are rarely harmed. Disputes outside the breeding season are usually over control of a food source.

Voice of authority
Listen out for the laugh-like "yaffle" call of the Green Woodpecker – a sure sign that a male is patrolling his territory.

Singing

Many species of garden bird have an incredibly varied and musical repertoire – an added incentive to attract birds to your garden. Birdsong escalates in spring as each species adds its distinctive song to the chorus, and the battle for mates and territories commences.

Why birds sing

Watching a bird such as a Song Thrush singing, it is easy to believe it is doing it just for fun. However, singing has a serious purpose. Chiefly a male activity, it is an essential mechanism for attracting a mate and luring females from afar. A good, strong vocal performance is a sign of a healthy male and an attractive mate. Singing is also used for marking and defending territorial boundaries. Song is a very effective way of warning other birds in the area to stay away.

Song and species

Listen to the birds in your garden and you should be able to pick out a variety of different songs – each bird produces its own unique sound. There are many recordings available that will help you learn

Popular song
The Blackbird has a mellow, fluty song. Its simple but melodic sound is a firm favourite with many people.

SPOTS FOR SINGING

Birds often use exactly the same perches from which to sing, referred to as song posts. Prominent places such as roof tops, the tops of bushes, trees, and fence posts are ideal, as the sound carries over long distances. Such behaviour means that you can enjoy the same birds regularly performing songs within a particular area.

Long-distance song
The Song Thrush has a far-carrying song. It often sings from gate posts and television aerials.

each species' distinct song. From the explosive trill of the Wren, to the varied repertoire of the Starling – which even includes mimicking telephones and road drills – and the barely audible squeaking of the tiny Goldcrest, with practice you will learn to recognize distinct songs.

Seasonal song

Birdsong becomes increasingly evident in spring. After an initial "tuning up" period during which birds produce a subsong – a muted, disjointed type of song – birds soon find their voices. By late spring, the dawn chorus provides an uplifting start to the day. You can sense each bird's desire to have its voice heard. Autumn and winter are quiet times for birdsong – the voice you are most likely to hear is the wistful warble of the Robin.

Dusk melodies
Birdsong can continue well into the evening, as this Blue Tit illustrates. There is often a resurgence in song at this time, after a break in the middle part of the day.

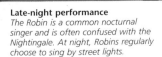

Late-night performance
The Robin is a common nocturnal singer and is often confused with the Nightingale. At night, Robins regularly choose to sing by street lights.

Courtship

Male birds have to complete many tasks to ensure they breed successfully, and securing a relationship is vital. There are courtship displays to perform and regular bonding activities to undertake before male and female accept one other and begin to rear a family.

Courtship displays

Many birds perform visual displays to make sure they attract the attention of potential mates and rivals. As with songs, different species have distinct styles of display. They may show off their colourful plumage, puff out their feathers to seem larger, or perform elaborate flight displays. Making themselves so obvious carries the risk of being seen by predators, but mating successfully makes the risk worthwhile.

Choosing a partner

Some birds pair only for a single breeding season. Others pair for longer and merely have to renew their bonds every year when they return to the same area to breed. In such cases, courtship is rapid because of this familiarity. Mature, experienced birds make the best parents, and older males are the most skilled at attracting mates. Females consider all of the attributes each prospective male has to offer, but prefer an older mate.

Courtship gift
This male Blue Tit (left) is presenting a female with a gift of food to seal their relationship and prove he is a suitable mate.

Mating dance
During courtship, Dunnocks perform a distinct visual display – shaking their wings while singing – all done in an effort to impress a potential mate.

Preparing to mate

After the initial attraction resulting from singing and displaying, pairs of birds become much closer. The male presents his partner with gifts, in the form of food. This aids the bonding process, but may also prove to the female that he will be a good provider for her during the incubation period and for future young. Mutual preening is another important part of courtship and you can often see pairs of birds preening one another in spring. Once the courting and bonding process is complete, and male and female have accepted each other, and the breeding territory, the pair move on to nesting.

Both birds may become less visible at this point as they do not want to make themselves obvious to predators as they set about raising a family.

Nesting and rearing

The nesting season is a busy time for birds and an exciting time for garden birdwatchers. Breeding successfully is a challenge that every mature bird must rise to every year.

The nesting season

Birds have to reproduce to maintain their numbers and compensate for the inevitable natural losses that occur. Some garden birds can raise as many as four broods in a year.

The nesting season for garden birds lasts from about March to August. Some birds may nest earlier in mild winters. Multi-brooded species, and birds that have suffered a nesting failure may complete their nesting cycle slightly later. Flexibility is the key to coping with the unpredictable weather that occurs in the UK during spring and summer.

Birds nest in this period because there is plenty of natural cover to nest in and an abundance of insect food. The increased daylight hours allow sufficient time to find enough nutrition for the entire family.

Early-nesting bird
Mistle Thrushes are early nesters and this species often builds its nest in the fork of a tree.

Nest construction

Each bird has a unique style of nest and uses different construction materials, which include vegetation, mud, hair, moss, and cobwebs.

Birds nest in a variety of locations, and many garden birds use nest boxes. Some birds build multiple nests and then select the most suitable one to use.

It is vital to select a safe nest site, concealed from predators and sheltered from the elements, as this ensures the best chance of successfully rearing a brood.

In spring, you may see birds gathering beakfuls of grass, vegetation, and mud, which is a sign that they are nesting in, or near, your garden. Assist their efforts by suspending wool and hair from trees, bushes, or a washing line, and maintain a puddle of wet mud in hot, dry weather.

Greenfinch nest
Greenfinches construct their neat, cup-shaped nests in the thickest parts of trees.

Blue Tit nest
Blue Tits build nests in natural cavities such as tree-holes, and also like hole-fronted nest boxes.

Long-tailed Tit nest
Long-tailed Tits make sealed, ball-shaped nests from spiders' webs, moss, and lichens.

Eggs and laying

Once the nest is ready and the pair have mated, the female lays her eggs. She lays one per day because of the strain it places on her body and resources.

A clutch is the total number of eggs laid and incubated at one time, and is dependent on the species. Clutch size also varies within species, depending on the female's condition, food availability, and the weather.

The parent birds incubate the eggs to keep them warm – usually a job for the female. Incubation starts when the clutch is complete so that the eggs hatch at the same time. The incubation period varies between species. Once the eggs have hatched, the adults' work

Nest repairs
A House Sparrow typically builds an untidy nest with materials such as hair and feathers. Nests may need repairs during the season.

intensifies. They have to brood (sit on) the nestlings to keep them warm as chicks cannot maintain their own body temperature, and provide them with food.

The chicks are demanding and need feeding on a very regular basis. Blue Tits make several hundred visits to their nest every day with food to satisfy the appetites of their chicks.

Hatching
Breaking out of an egg is not easy for a tiny chick. A special, hard "egg tooth" on its beak helps the chick smash its way out.

Shell

Egg tooth

Wing

Feeding the nestlings
This female Green Woodpecker is feeding an expectant juvenile. Young birds grow at a rapid pace and must be fed frequently.

Leaving the nest

Parents encourage chicks to leave the nest by bringing them less food. Once chicks are fully grown and fully feathered, they fly the nest and become fledglings.

A fledgling's maiden flight could go smoothly or end in a crash landing. Pride-denting experiences are all part of the learning process for juvenile birds.

Parents still bring food to their young for a time after they have left the nest. Some species learn to fend for themselves very quickly. House Sparrows are independent within a week of leaving the nest, allowing the parents to take a well-deserved rest, or prepare to start a new brood.

ABANDONED BIRDS

Young birds often look lost and vulnerable, but remember that the parents are probably not far away. Fledglings of species such as Robins, Collared Doves, Woodpigeons, and thrushes spend a day or two on the ground before they can fly. In most cases, the birds will be fine, so resist the urge to go to their aid.

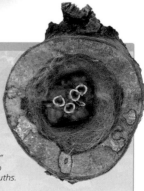

Baby birds
The colourful "gapes" encourage parents to put food in their mouths.

Migration

Birds earn our admiration through their ability to fly. Those that migrate, undergoing incredible, globe-spanning journeys that cover thousands of miles, are truly awe-inspiring. Some birds fly to the UK from as far away as South Africa.

Why they do it

Migration stretches birds to the limits of their endurance and leaves them seriously undernourished. So why do it? Summer visitors migrate to Britain and Europe because of the abundance of food and nesting sites in the northern hemisphere.

Winter visitors migrate to escape the icy, food-deprived environs of northern Europe. Gardens in the UK are sanctuaries for vast numbers of finches and thrushes from Scandinavia and Russian Starlings. Timing is vital for spring arrivals such as Swifts and House Martins.

Mass flight
Millions of Starlings from Eastern Europe and Russia flock to Britain for the winter.

Welcome nourishment
Here a Fieldfare eats windfall fruit, which can be a lifesaver in hard weather. Field-fares come to the UK in late autumn.

Arrive early and there may not be enough insect food. Arrive late and the best territory will be taken. The benefits of migration outweigh the detriments. It is a risk that many birds have to take to survive.

How they do it

There are many unanswered questions as to how birds migrate with such accuracy. One of the greatest feats of migration is performed by young birds, which instinctively know when to migrate and exactly where to go. To prepare, some species put on as much extra body fat as possible for the journey, without compromising their ability to fly. Regular routes are followed and major landmarks, for example rivers, provide natural markers to guide birds on their way. Once they have reached their destination, birds must replenish the fat supplies used on the journey.

Long-haul flier
The Swallow flies all the way from Africa to feast on insects and nest in barns and outhouses in the UK and Europe. Adults return to the same nesting sites every spring.

Feeding

Feeding is an everyday necessity for birds. Birds will eat both the food you provide for them and food that is naturally available, such as insects. Each species has its own dietary requirements and has adapted to find and eat different foods.

Importance of feeding

In spring, birds endure numerous stresses. Feeding on the right food, and plenty of it, is vital. In summer, natural insect food is ample, but there are extra mouths to feed – providing the right food for adults and young at this time does birds a great service. In autumn, fewer birds will make use of your garden as they take advantage of the

Balancing act
This Blue Tit is using its acrobatic skills and excellent sense of balance to feast on a fallen apple.

Natural food supply
A Song Thrush will turn its head to one side to help spot worms in the soil below before extracting one to eat.

abundance of food available in the countryside. Winter is the most important time to feed garden birds. Natural food is scarce and sudden cold snaps can leave birds tired, hungry, and in need of our help.

Methods of feeding

Every species of garden bird has a particular diet and favoured meal items, and is equipped to find and eat different foods. Beak shape varies by family, from seed-crushing beaks (as with chunky-beaked finches) to insect-catching beaks (as with "tweezer-beaked" Swallows). It is interesting to watch the ways in which different species use their beaks to feed.

Natural foraging

A large percentage of a bird's time is spent searching for food. This uses up valuable energy. Having access to a reliable and large supply of food (such as a well-stocked garden) means that less effort and time is required for foraging.

Some birds search for food over a wide area and may visit several gardens as part of a circuit. Aerial insect eaters, for example Swifts, patrol the same area of sky, snapping up flies in their beaks.

Agile eater
Nuthatches wedge acorns into the bark of trees and use their chisel-like beaks to hammer them open. Their beaks are also used to dig insects out of bark.

HOARDING FOOD

Certain garden birds are excellent hoarders of food. Watch out for Coal Tits and Jays coming to your feeders and flying off with peanuts. This is common behaviour in autumn when they carry off their bounty to secret stashes, which they can call upon during the hard times of winter.

Accidental planters
Jays aid in the regener-ation of woodland. Acorns they forget to collect from their underground larders can germinate into oak trees.

1 **Food**
It is important to provide bird food in spring. It may seem as if the toughest time of winter is over, but a shortage of natural food occurs in March and April.

2 **Shelter**
Have you provided somewhere for birds to nest? Nest boxes are easy to erect, but you could also provide natural cover in the form of trees and bushes.

3 **Cover**
Birds are preoccupied with breeding in spring, making them vulnerable to predators. Ensure birdfeeders are placed near cover.

Spring

When spring arrives, there is a buzz of activity in the garden from dawn until dusk. Birdsong fills the air, displays are performed to attract mates, and breeding territories are claimed.

Nesting on their mind

At the start of spring, birds begin to prepare for the most important activity of the year – nesting. Firstly, they have to get into peak condition to meet the physical demands of defending a territory and attracting a mate. Many garden birds take on a fresh new breeding plumage and look more colourful than they did in winter.

Spring arrivals

It is all change in the garden in spring. Some of the birds that spent winter in your garden will disperse to breeding territories elsewhere, while others arrive in spring to breed. Migrants from Africa, such as Swifts and House Martins, begin to appear in gardens in April and May.

VITAL SPRING FOOD

In spring, birds need nutritious food to provide enough energy to complete the many tasks they have at this time of year. Nyjer seeds, sunflower seeds, raisins, and sultanas will all be popular, and very beneficial to birds.

SPRING BIRD PLUMAGE

PIED WAGTAIL

Black and white with long tail

STARLING

Black and speckled with an iridescent sheen

BULLFINCH

Males are red below with a black cap

Noisy neighbour
The "drumming" noise produced by the Great Spotted Woodpecker is created by hammering its strong beak and reinforced skull against a tree.

■ **SEASONAL TIPS**
There is much to enjoy about the garden in spring, as well as plenty of "bird gardening" to keep you busy.

1 **Predator watch**
Young birds start to appear around the garden and "squeak" from flower beds and within bushes – keep cats at bay to help them stay safe.

2 **Water**
Provide water for your garden birds. Natural supplies dry up in hot summers, and even a small puddle will be gratefully received.

3 **Food caution**
Young birds can choke on large food items, so make sure everything you put out is in small, manageable pieces that will not swell up inside them.

Summer

We may enjoy relaxing in the garden on summer days, but garden birds are busy tending to the needs of their demanding broods. Young birds are often entertaining to watch.

Baby boom

It is exciting to see the first young birds of the year in your garden, and a relief that birds you have become familiar with have bred successfully. Scaly, short-tailed young Blackbirds are often the first to appear. Female birds that have been missing for weeks will reappear, now that they do not have to brood eggs or young.

Worn out

In contrast to freshly feathered youngsters, adult birds may look scruffy by summer, with worn plumage and missing feathers. They have less time to look after their plumage while tending to their young, so their appearance suffers. Finding food for the young also takes its toll.

A HELPING HAND

Parent birds can struggle to find enough food for their young. Assist their efforts by putting out mealworms or waxworms. Place them in a steep-sided tray and adults will carry the worms to their young, ensuring a nutritious meal.

SPRING BIRD PLUMAGE

HOUSE MARTIN

White below and glossy blue above

HOUSE SPARROW
Males have a black bib and grey crown

GREENFINCH
Males are green with yellow wing flashes

Colourful visitor
The male Chaffinch is a handsome sight. Provide seed and shrubs and bushes for cover and this finch may become a resident in your garden.

Autumn

In autumn the breeding season is over, young birds are independent, and birds recuperate from the stresses of the summer. Parents and young go their separate ways, but all are aware that winter is approaching.

■ **SEASONAL TIPS**
It may seem as if birds don't need our help as much in autumn, but now is the time to do a bit of housekeeping.

1 Portion control
If you find that a surplus of food remains in your feeders, this is a suitable time to reduce the amount of food you put out for birds.

2 Sanitize
With the breeding season over, you should clean out any nest boxes in your garden with warm, soapy water to prevent the spread of disease.

3 Prepare
Autumn is a good time to purchase and site new feeders. Also, put in any orders for bird food, as the harsh days of winter are quickly approaching.

Changing times

This is the season when adults moult their old, tatty feathers and replace them with fresh ones. Many birds will go to ground for a time while they do this. They must remain hidden from predators while they are vulnerable. Young birds are moulting too, and start to look more like their parents as they attain adult-like feathers.

Stocking up

It is important for birds to stock up on food while it is easy to find. As autumn progresses, birds gain valuable extra weight. You will also see flocks of birds forming. These gatherings may stay together until the following spring.

THE NATURAL HARVEST

In autumn, food is relatively easy to find in the countryside. Hedgerows are full of berries, orchards have fruit, and wildflowers are setting seed in meadows. Fewer birds may visit your garden at this time, but they will return soon.

AUTUMN BIRD PLUMAGE

GOLDCREST
Yellow crown
White wing bars

GOLDFINCH
Yellow wing bars

COAL TIT
White nape patch and buff below

Autumn colour
Unusual visitors, such as this colourful and unmistakable Jay, may visit your garden in autumn as birds disperse from their place of birth.

■ SEASONAL TIPS
Look after birds in winter and you will be rewarded with regular visits by a variety of grateful species.

1 **Constant supply**
Make sure food and water are always available. Birds cannot afford to waste valuable time and energy visiting an empty garden.

2 **Daily top up**
Fill your feeders and top up your water supplies at the beginning and end of each day, as this is when birds urgently need sustenance.

3 **Ice-free supplies**
Keep your bird tables, feeders, and water supplies free of snow and ice. These can hamper access to vital supplies of food and water.

Winter

Birds face a battle for survival during winter. Days are short and nights are long and cold. Natural food is scarce, so stock your garden with plenty of nutritious food for birds to feed on.

Feeding frenzy

Birds must eat regularly and well to survive in winter. The cold weather is not a problem as feathers provide excellent insulation, but being able to find enough food is the difference between life and death. Birds spend the vast majority of daylight hours feeding to build up sufficient fat reserves to survive the night.

Coming in from the cold

Your resident garden birds will be a regular sight in winter, but you may also spot birds from further afield. Many birds seek sanctuary in gardens as food dwindles in the countryside. You may also spot winter migrants such as Redwings, Fieldfares, Bramblings, and Siskins.

VITAL WINTER FOOD

This is the time to provide birds with high-energy foods such as suet bars, fat balls, and bird cakes laced with nuts, seed, and dried fruit. By the start of winter, much of the natural supply of fruit and berries will have been eaten.

WINTER BIRD PLUMAGE

BLACKCAP

Cap is black on males, brown on females

Brown back, speckled below

FIELDFARE

Black, white, and orange body

BRAMBLING

Winter insulation
This Robin has fluffed its feathers, trapping air for extra warmth. The arrival of hard winter weather brings tough times for our garden birds.

Birds in your garden

There are many simple steps you can take to encourage birds into your garden, such as providing food, water, and nest boxes, and adding bird-friendly plants.

The garden habitat

A well planned garden, managed with birds in mind, is as valuable for birds as parts of the countryside. Provide as many features as you can, from nesting cover to places to feed, and you can create your own private nature reserve.

Gardens are important

It is testimony to the value of gardens as wildlife habitats that so many birds are classed as "garden birds" despite the fact that they are also common residents of the countryside. Many birds seek sanctuary in the form of food and shelter in gardens, where they find respite from the icy grip of winter.

The climate can be unpredictable all year round in the UK and many birds, especially thrushes and finches, come into towns and cities during food shortages and spells of adverse weather.

Gardens also provide nesting sites for birds in spring and summer. Allowing birds access to the roof of your house creates a whole host of extra nesting opportunities. Gardens, and those who own them and cater for birds, provide an invaluable service.

Garden bird sanctuary
This garden is a haven for birds and provides everything they need – food, feeding places, and a variety of plants.

Garden offerings

Almost every garden provides benefits for birds at some stage of the year. Even gardens that are not managed with birds in mind can provide something for the quick-thinking and adaptive species of birds that are able to live alongside us. The smallest things can help birds out, from the seeds formed by a patch of weeds, to a place to nest in an overgrown bush. It is easy to build on such natural attractions and make a garden into a haven for birds all year.

A lawn provides insect eating, ground-feeding birds such as thrushes and Starlings with somewhere to feed. A perimeter hedge is a place to roost and nest, and flowerbeds a place to forage for seeds. Supplementary bird benefits, such as food, bird-baths, and nest boxes, will all add value to a garden.

The more varied you make your garden, the more useful it will be for birds. Aim to include as many natural and supplementary features as possible.

Moveable feast
Earthworms are a great source of food for garden birds. Encourage them by not using pesticides.

Water feature
A pond will provide drinking and bathing places for birds, as well as a home for all kinds of wetland wildlife.

Natural food source
Berry-bearing bushes are a valuable source of food for birds in the autumn and winter. Try to have at least one bush in your garden.

Shelter

The variety of birds that visit your garden, how they use it, and the length of time they spend there can all be influenced by the amount and type of shelter and cover that you provide.

Why is shelter important?

Sheltered environments are best for garden birds. No bird wants to be blasted by the wind or be seated on a feeder that blows back and forth like a pendulum. Birds look for a solid perch and protection from the elements. Putting some careful thought into laying out your garden will make it an attractive place for birds.

Shelter comes from natural sources, such as hedges, shrubs, and trees, as well as fences and walls – staple garden features – and sometimes even your house. You cannot control the direction or force of the wind, but you can

House guests
House Martins will build their mud-cup nests in a sheltered spot under the eaves of your house.

place your feeders, nest boxes, and bird baths in sheltered positions. Bushes also help to reduce the effects of the wind.

Birds visiting your garden will often arrive at the same time and follow a fixed pattern of behaviour. Flocks of birds will descend from a particular tree, bush, or fence and then drop onto feeders or the lawn to feed. They will get used to the layout of your garden and rely on certain bushes for escaping dangerous predators.

It is important that you plant feeders close to cover – so birds can fly into them if a cat or Sparrowhawk is on the prowl – but not so close that they cannot see danger creeping up unseen. Natural cover is a must for

Room to roost
Gardens with plenty of perching places will make birds feel safer when they come down to feed. Starlings usually arrive en masse.

attracting birds to nest in your garden. Nest boxes can be put on walls and fences (see p.24), but some cover nearby for extra perching points will increase the likelihood of them being occupied.

making good use of a hedge. One advantage of natural cover such as a hedge over a man-made structure is that it provides nesting opportunities and more perching places. The trees and shrubs in the

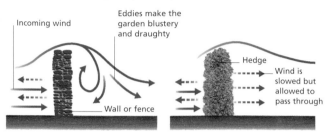

Incoming wind

Eddies make the garden blustery and draughty

Wall or fence

Hedge

Wind is slowed but allowed to pass through

Hedges and solid walls
By allowing some air to pass through them, hedges produce less turbulence than solid barriers such as walls.

How to provide shelter

The prevailing wind in most parts of the UK is from the southwest, and at any time of year wind speeds from the direction can get up to strong and even gale force on the Beaufort scale. Work out which direction is south and southwest in your garden, and either try to provide natural cover (see p.38) or position fences so they give shelter to birds.

You can reduce the effects of the wind by

hedge also provide food. See page 38 for more information about which species to plant for food.

If you have a wall or fence, grow climbers and shrubs up it as the two work well in tandem. You have the added advantage of providing shelter while the hedge grows.

Planting hedges
Use string and posts to mark out the position of your hedging plants and ensure a straight line.

Maintaining hedges
Prune your hedge and keep it under control. Avoid any maintenance during the spring and summer nesting season.

Natural food

By selecting trees, shrubs, climbers, and other plants that provide food for birds, and supplying supplementary food in bird feeders, you will ensure that your garden will be visited by a wide variety of birds throughout the year.

Trees

Trees provide an ideal perching spot for birds and a good source of natural food. Not all gardens can accommodate a mini-forest or large trees, but most should have space for at least one well-pruned tree.

Deciduous trees (those that lose their leaves in autumn) are the best ones to plant for resident garden birds. Many conifers are non-native and have limited wildlife value. Be sure to avoid Leylandii, a fast-growing, foundation-damaging, quick-to-die-back conifer that blocks out light from everything else around it. Many trees are a direct source of

Cold-weather food
Rowan, as well as hawthorn and guelder rose, provide the type of berries that Waxwings gobble up freely.

food, providing seeds, nuts, and berries. The cones of birches and alders offer seeds for species such as Goldfinches, Siskins, and Lesser Redpolls. Hazels produce nuts and rowans plump berries for thrushes and Waxwings during autumn and winter. Don't forget to plant apple, pear, and plum trees – thrushes and Starlings love fallen fruit.

The numerous insects that live in trees at different stages of their life cycle are another perennial source of natural food for birds. Caterpillars are great "baby food" for Blue and Great Tits in spring and summer.

Shrubs

Shrubs are the best source of natural food in gardens. Hawthorn and guelder rose are among the many that provide good crops of berries for garden birds like Blackbirds, and autumn and winter visitors such as Fieldfares and Redwings.

Shrubs are also home to a large variety of insects – even the smallest urban garden may be home to hundreds of different species, many of which are preferred by birds.

Nut larder
The hazel tree has delicate catkins – cylindrical flower clusters – and tasty nuts for birds in autumn and winter.

BE A MESSY GARDENER

Try not to be too tidy when gardening. Let some grass grow long, and leave a patch of wildflowers – they provide seeds and attract insects for birds to eat. Don't trim back shrubs too early, and leave berries intact as a food source throughout winter. Avoid chemical pesticides – birds provide natural pest control.

Watch out for warblers, and tits picking off insects on and under leaves and working the branches to probe into crevices.

The best shrubs provide nesting sites and food. The hawthorn and blackthorn – common countryside plants that look good in gardens too – are excellent hedging plants. They can also be grown individually.

It is best to grow a mix of shrubs, whether you plant them as hedges or individually. The more species you grow, the wider the variety of food you provide.

In summer, when many birds start to include insects in their diet, having natural food on hand is a must. Birds will use the food that you put out in feeders, but they like to feed protein-rich insects to their young.

Food and cover
Multi-stemmed shrubs, such as dogwood, create good cover for birds and provide winter food in the form of berries (right).

Versatile blackthorn
The blackthorn provides nesting sites, and its berries are a source of food for birds in autumn and winter.

Winter favourite
Red berries are an irresistible draw for fruit-loving birds. A cotoneaster will be steadily stripped of its berries by birds.

»

Copying nature
Try to create natural profiles in your garden similar to the natural woodland edge shown here. Curved edges make hedges longer, with more room for wildlife.

Climbers

Ivy is often seen as an unwelcome climber in gardens, growing fast and covering walls and fences, but for birds it is hard to beat. It not only provides plenty of cover, but its flowers attract insects in late summer and autumn, and the berries are a source of food through winter. Do let some ivy grow – you can control it as required and keep it in check. Blackbirds, Robins, and several other garden residents like to nest in ivy.

Honeysuckle is another good choice, not only for its sweet-smelling flowers that attract insects, but also for the cover it provides. Although honeysuckle

loses its leaves later on in the year, reducing available cover, it does hang on to them well into autumn. Its stems grow densely, creating good roosting habitats in winter and nesting sites in summer. House Sparrows like to roost in mature honeysuckle.

Climbers also help in concealing holes in fences and chipped and cracked bricks, and they can also add stability to wobbly fences.

Small plants

Many wildflowers look great in the garden, offering a variety of flower

Multi-tasking plants
Plant a nectar-rich flower border like this one to encourage insects. A native wildflower mix will bear seeds for birds.

Woody climber
Wisteria is a good climber for growing against walls and provides strong support for birds' nests.

shapes and colour, and structural diversity – from low-growing plants to tall ones that birds can perch on. Being native, these plants play host to more insects than others whose natural range is outside the UK.

Small plants are also a good source of seeds, supplying food to birds throughout winter. Goldfinches extract the seeds of teasels as they balance on the spiky flowerheads in autumn and winter. Thistles are also a perennial favourite with this sought-after species. Sunflowers are best grown up against a fence or wall using

Log piles
Leaving a pile of logs in a shaded corner will make sure you provide a home for insects that feed on rotting wood.

Protein source
Fieldfares and other thrushes make use of lawns as a good source of protein-rich worms.

stakes – they can shoot up to more than 2.5 m (8 ft). You can leave them to produce seeds and let Greenfinches and other birds extract the seeds in autumn themselves. The other option is to gather the seeds and leave them in your feeders and on bird tables in winter, when food is scarce.

Other excellent plants for attracting insects

include red campion, cornflower, foxglove, and cowslip.

Don't be afraid to pack plants into borders and beds as this provides a good habitat for insects. You can always thin them out if required. Make sure you have the right balance of species. By researching the flowering times of different species, you can ensure a continuous supply of nectar in your garden from early spring to autumn.

Supporting animals
The rotting vegetation in a compost bin supports worms, insects, and other animals that will, in turn, attract birds.

Types of food

You can buy all kinds of safe and nutritious food for your garden birds. There is a wide variety of tasty treats available – from the most popular individual seeds and specially formulated seed mixes to bird puddings and mealworms.

Seeds and seed mixes

Seed mixes are available for feeders and bird tables. The RSPB offers a wide variety of high-quality specialized mixes, some of which are formulated for specific seasons. Key ingredients include millet, flaked maize, and sunflower seeds. Some mixes have sultanas, raisins, and flaked oats.

Black sunflower seeds are an excellent year-round food. This variety has a higher oil content than the striped seeds and is more nutritious. Sunflower hearts (the husked kernels) are a popular no-mess food. Pinhead oatmeal is another year-round staple. Also try mealworms and nyjer seeds, both of which are very popular with garden birds.

Experiment and see what kinds of food your garden birds prefer. Putting out a variety of foods will increase your chances of attracting more species to your garden.

Attracting visitors
Sunflower hearts in a hanging mesh feeder will ensure a steady flow of birds, including Robins (left) and Goldfinches (right).

Sunflower hearts
Hearts save you the trouble of clearing up inedible shells and are easy for birds to eat. They are rich in oil and protein.

Nyjer seeds
Oil-rich and highly nutritious seeds for Goldfinches, Lesser Redpolls, and Siskins, nyjer must be served in special feeders because it is so small.

No-mess sunflower mix
This no-waste, no-mess blend of sunflower hearts, kibbled maize, husk-free oats, and canary seed suits all feeders.

Feeder mix
This is a nutritious mix of oil-rich black and striped sunflower seeds, husk-free oats, and canary seeds.

Feeder mix extra
Added protein and energy from sunflower hearts combine with sunflower seeds, husk-free oats, red millet, and canary seed in this mix.

Sunflower seeds with shells
Cheaper than hearts, and high in energy-giving oils, these seeds can be put out on tables or in feeders.

Table mix
This mix contains black and striped sunflower seeds, sunflower hearts, husk-free oats, kibbled maize, and wheat.

Table mix extra
High proportions of smaller and husk-free seeds – such as sunflower hearts, oats, and millet – make this mix easy to eat. They also provide extra energy.

Ground mix
This shell-less, maximum-energy mix of sunflower hearts, raisins, husk-free oats, and flaked maize is best for ground-feeding birds.

»

Suet and fat

A wide range of excellent, high-energy winter foods containing suet and fat is available. This includes suet balls and other fat-based bird cakes, nibbles, and sprinkles with extras, either loose with the pellets or within the suet mix.

Suet cake
Cakes can be hung in special flat, hanging feeders to make them last longer.

Suet balls
These can be hung individually or placed in heaps of three or four balls in a hanging mesh feeder.

Suet sprinkles
Sprinkles can come with insects, berries, or mealworms. These easy-to-feed pellets are ideal for bird feeders.

Insects and worms

Available in live and dried forms, insects and worms are highly nutritious recent additions to the bird-food market. These, together with traditional staples such as seeds, can ensure your garden birds have a balanced diet.

Live mealworms
These beetle larvae can be handled cleanly. High in protein, they are an excellent choice for young birds.

Dried mealworms
Although this food has the goodness of live mealworms, it lacks the moisture. Sprinkle the dried worms or soak them in warm water.

Bugs 'n' bits
This blend of dried mealworms, waterfly, and river shrimp is sprinkled on bird tables or on the ground and mixed with seeds.

Other food

The menu for your garden birds does not stop at the available range of specialist mixes. Leftovers or surplus food from your own kitchen can still provide nutritious food for a wide variety of species. It is vital to avoid serving any mouldy or stale foods. Also, make sure you are aware of how specific food items affect other creatures that use your garden. Shown below are some more bird foods to add to the diet of your garden birds.

Blue Tit feeding on coconut
A halved coconut used as a suet holder may attract agile birds such as tits.

Fresh coconut
Hang up a fresh coconut after breaking it in half. Rinse out the residue of coconut water to prevent mildew.

Uncooked porridge oats
This is a favourite with many birds. Never serve cooked porridge oats though – they could harden around birds' beaks.

Raisins
Though a fruity treat for a variety of birds, raisins are toxic to dogs.

Cooked rice
Brown or white rice is a good choice for birds, but it must not be salted.

Feeders

Catering for the varied feeding requirements of garden birds will increase the number of species that visit your garden. Regularly stock your feeders throughout the year and you will be treated to a constant procession of birds coming to feed.

Bird tables

Bird tables are an efficient way of providing food for birds and are a feature of many bird-friendly gardens. A variety of bird table styles and designs are available, but the basic elements are a flat serving area, which should have adequate drainage to prevent food from becoming waterlogged, and raised edges to keep food from blowing away. Bird tables allow several birds to feed simultaneously.

The elevated nature of bird tables protects birds from cats, keeps food off the ground, and allows you to observe garden birds with ease. Birds also feel safe at bird tables because they can see predators approaching.

Low bird table
Both ground-feeding species and birds that also feed at higher levels, such as the Blue Tits and Great Tits shown here, are attracted to low bird tables.

Covered bird table
This pole-mounted bird table has a sturdy base and a roof to keep food dry. The tray is removable for easy cleaning.

Ground feeders

Serving food at ground level is important for those birds that are less comfortable at bird tables and hanging feeders. For example, the Song Thrush and Dunnock are two species that are rare at elevated feeders, but will readily come to food at ground level.

Ground feeders are also excellent for species such as the Wren, which is timid in communal feeding situations.

You can put food directly on the ground and scatter it widely, but it is worth noting that it can spoil quickly and may attract rodents such as rats and squirrels. Specially-designed low bird tables or hoppers solve these potential problems.

Ground-feeder protector
A folding cage placed over a ground feeder protects birds from cats and other predators as they feed.

HYGIENE ALERT

Regularly scrape off old food from bird tables and the ground below. Clean the entire table and the floor beneath it with a mild detergent to prevent droppings and disease accumulating.

Hanging feeders

Birds naturally hang from trees and bushes as they search for food, so coming to a hanging feeder is second nature for many. Several species of bird have enough agility to cling to hanging feeders, while birds that aren't naturally agile, such as Starlings and Robins, have learned how to adapt.

Hanging feeders protect food from rodents and eliminate the risk of a cat attack. Like bird tables, they are a must for any bird garden.

Tubular feeders are perfect for supplying seeds. They usually have several feeding portholes, which have perches for birds to grip onto.

Some feeders come with a screw thread, allowing them to be mounted onto poles – perfect for places where hanging positions are

limited. You can also attach trays to the pole to catch any fallen seeds. Another type of feeder is a hanging cage, which is ideal for bird cake.

> **HYGIENE ALERT**
>
> Keep your birds healthy and prevent disease by cleaning feeders regularly with a mild detergent and a bristle brush. Move your feeders periodically to prevent a build up of droppings.

Tubular seed feeder
This seed feeder (right) has multiple perches and portholes to allow several birds, in this case Greenfinches and a Great Tit, to feed at once.

Nyjer seed feeder
These small seeds are best provided in a specialized feeder with small portholes to reduce the amount of wasted seed.

Specialist feeders

Squirrels can be an unwelcome visitor to birdfeeders, but there are several innovations to deter them, and stop them from destroying your feeders with their sharp teeth.

Feeder guardians are wire cages that are resistant to squirrel attacks. These can be easily fitted over feeders, allowing small birds to feed. Plastic domed baffles fitted around feeder poles make it difficult for squirrels to get to the food at the top.

There are pole-mounted versions of bird tables and hanging feeders, and you can place seed trays around the poles to prevent food spillage, and

Feeder guardian
The wire cage on this squirrel-proof feeder will deter grey squirrels, but still allow smaller birds, such as these tits, to come and feed.

give birds an additional feeding station. Special nyjer feeders, which are similar to hanging feeders – may tempt the colourful Goldfinch and other finches into your garden.

Suction-cup window feeder
This feeder will quickly and easily attach to any window, providing an excellent view of birds as they feed.

Siting feeders

Consider the position from which you would like to watch the birds when siting your feeders.

Feeder placement
With a bit of planning, you can position several types of feeder around your garden. If a feeder proves unpopular with the birds, move it around until you find a more suitable site.

Siting feeders

Give careful consideration to the placement of feeders in your garden. You must ensure that birds can find the food easily, but are also safe from predators. You will also want a good view of the feeders, so you can watch the birds without disturbing them. Bear all of these points in mind before you put up a new feeder.

Birds need to have a clear all-round view because they could be taken by surprise by a cat or Sparrowhawk while their minds are occupied with feeding. They also need cover nearby so that they can make a dash for safety if necessary. The ideal scenario is to place bird tables no more than 2–3m from cover.

Bird tables can also be suspended from tree branches via secure chains.

Timid species such as Dunnocks will use low bird tables. Place them close to cover so the birds feel secure.

Wall feeder
Bird tables like this one can be mounted to walls. Make sure they are not too near the roof line where cats or other predators could lurk.

KEY

☐ Ground feeders
☐ Bird tables
☐ Hanging feeders

A caged feeder at ground level is best positioned in an exposed spot so that birds can see predators approaching.

For a good view of the birds coming to your bird table, place it close to your house.

Pole-mounted feeders are easily moved, so find the birds' favoured spot.

Hanging tube feeders can be suspended from tree branches. Ensure threats are minimized.

Easy, natural feeder
Rub food into the cracks of a log, as shown here, to make a rustic feeder.

BIRDFEEDER THREATS

Cats pose one of the biggest threats to the safety of garden birds. They kill millions of birds every year in the UK. You can help to keep the birds in your garden safe by putting careful thought into where you position your feeders and encourage birds to feed. Sonar devices and prickly bushes are good cat deterrents.

Natural predator
Help to alert birds to an approaching cat by fitting a small bell to its quick-release collar.

Making food

You can use your own culinary skills to provide food for birds to complement the specialist bird food you buy. Many of your leftovers will be gratefully accepted by birds, so consider this before you reach for the dustbin.

Making your own bird cake

Give your garden birds a treat and make them a cake. Mix seed, unsalted, chopped peanuts, small pieces of fruit, and kitchen leftovers (see opposite) with melted suet or lard in a saucepan. Fashion the mix into ball shapes, bars, and cakes with the aid of moulds.

Let the cake set and then hang it up on a hook, or place in a cage feeder. Bird cakes are a great way of giving your birds the energy they need to survive in hard weather.

Quick feeder
You can put bird cake mix and suet into the cracks and crevices of hanging logs.

Using your leftovers

Many kitchen scraps provide excellent, nutritious food for garden birds. They are great additions to the bird table and will soon attract a wide variety of birds. Important items to avoid are salty, spicy, and mouldy foods, unsaturated fats, cooked porridge oats,

Valuable food source
Birds are not too proud or fussy to take advantage of our leftovers. Many garden birds, including Blackbirds, will eat kitchen scraps.

although these are fine raw, and desiccated coconut, which can swell up inside a bird's stomach.

Some of the foods that birds love and that are often thrown away at meal times are illustrated below. All of these are of value to birds, particularly in winter when natural food is hard to find. Supplementing the specialist bird food you buy with kitchen leftovers also helps to keep the costs of your bird garden down, and further varies the diet of your garden birds.

Outdoor dining
This Robin is enjoying some leftover bread. Bird tables are the ideal place to put out scraps such as old vegetables.

Bacon rind
The rind from unsalted bacon and other cuts of meat should be cut into manageable pieces.

Cheese
Stale (but not mouldy) cheese can be grated and put out for birds. It is rich in protein.

Potatoes
Cooked potatoes are a regular leftover, which can be put to good use on the bird table.

Cake
Cake is fine for birds, but only put out small amounts, as it is not particularly nutritious.

Rice
Cooked, unflavoured rice is a popular bird table treat. It is a particular favourite of Starlings.

Fruit
Any fruit that is starting to soften or brown will make a fine meal for birds.

Water

It is easy to concentrate on providing food for birds and forget that water is equally important. Birds need to drink regularly, and keeping their plumage in tip-top condition requires regular baths.

Keeping clean
It is entertaining to watch birds, such as this Jay, take a bath. They are meticulous in their grooming.

Drinking

Birds need access to a clean supply of fresh water throughout the year. Natural supplies can start to run dry in hot summers, and during winter access to fresh water can be blocked by ice. It is especially important to remember to provide water at these times. The birds that you provide food for will also visit your water supply.

Bathing

Keeping feathers free from dust and dirt is important for birds, as it ensures they maintain their ability to fly. Birds must make sure their feathers do not become too wet and render them flightless and vulnerable to predators – to avoid this they flick water over themselves. Birds are communal bathers and you may be able to watch several species bathing together.

How to provide water

A birdbath is an attractive addition to your garden, but you can also place plant pot saucers in the ground or opt for a pond. Ensure birds have an all-round view and use shallow vessels to avoid drowning. Provide only clean, fresh water and change it regularly. Don't use chemicals to clean birdbaths, and defrost them in winter using hot water.

Easy access
Shallow edges enable birds, such as this Greenfinch, to come and drink with their feet still firmly on the ground.

Bathing in safety
An elevated birdbath allows you to watch birds easily and keeps them safe from marauding cats.

Nest boxes

The easiest way to encourage birds to nest in your garden is to provide nest boxes. Because natural nesting sites such as holes in old trees and hedgerows are now less common, they provide valuable nesting sites for many birds.

Open nest boxes

There are two main types of nest box, and each used by a different set of birds. To give yourself the best chance of attracting tenants, think about which birds you currently see on a regular basis in, or near, your garden.

The first major style of nest box is the open-fronted variety, which is either a half-open or completely open design. This style is used by Robins, Wrens, and Spotted Flycatchers, and less frequently by Blackbirds.

Safe haven
This simple construction has one half of the front panel cut away, allowing the birds to enter and leave with ease.

Open-fronted boxes are well ventilated and easy to clean. They provide birds with a safe place to raise a brood and to roost.

Closed nest boxes

The hole-fronted nest box is popular with Blue and Great Tits because it mimics the holes in trees that they use as natural nest sites. The size of the entrance hole varies for different species, from a 25mm diameter for Blue Tits, a 45mm opening for Starlings, and up to a 150mm opening for Tawny Owls. Several other species regularly use hole-fronted nest boxes, including Nuthatches, Coal Tits, and House Sparrows.

Classic design
The size of the nest box hole determines which species will nest in it. House Sparrows favour this design.

Other boxes

New nest box innovations include boxes for House Martins, which are placed under the eaves of a house, and internal boxes for Swifts, which can be used in areas such as lofts. Fewer modern buildings allow space for these birds to nest, so you will be doing them a great service if you do erect a box for them.

Sparrow terraces capitalize on the House Sparrow's colonial nature. If you have a large garden with a mature tree, you could put up a tea chest-type box for tawny owls.

Modern design
A removable front panel allows this nest box to be easily cleaned out after the breeding season has ended.

Well-concealed home
This hole-fronted nest box has a 25mm diameter opening to attract Blue Tits, and has been thoughtfully positioned within concealing ivy.

HYGIENE ALERT

Clean your nest boxes from August onwards, once the birds have stopped using them. Discard old nests and use boiling water to kill any remaining parasites. Let the box dry completely before replacing the lid.

Making nest boxes

Making a nest box for your garden is easy, fun, and can be very rewarding. Your efforts will be much appreciated by garden birds, and you will be delighted to discover that a box you have made has been selected and occupied by a family of nesting birds.

Building a home

It is possible to make your own version of both the open-fronted and hole-fronted style of nest box. It is not as difficult as you might think, as shown by the basic plan on the opposite page.

DIY nest box building is also a cheap way of providing valuable nesting sites for your garden birds. The materials you will need are weatherproof wood, galvanized nails and screws, and a hinge or strip of rubber for the lid.

Different bird species require holes of different diameters, for example: 25mm for Blue and Coal tits; 28mm for Great Tits; 32mm for House Sparrows; 45mm for Starlings; and 50mm for Great Spotted Woodpeckers.

The inside wall of the box, below the entrance hole, should have a rough texture to help the young birds to clamber up when it is time for them to leave.

Face the box between north and east to avoid strong sunlight and wet winds, and tilt it slightly forwards to keep the rain off. Hole-fronted boxes should be positioned at a height of 2–4m.

Selective entrance
Open-fronted boxes should be placed at a height of 2–4m for Spotted Flycatchers, and less than 2m high for other species of bird.

Natural home
Your homemade nest box w: soon blend in and become part of your garden's natu: surroundings (left).

HOW TO BUILD A NEST BOX

Use the dimensions shown to mark and cut the wooden panels. Mark out the entrance hole using a compass and carefully cut it out. The metal plate deters predators. Use 38mm galvanized screws and nails to fix the panels together, and leave the wood used for the box untreated for the safety of the birds.

Materials

❶ 15mm thick floorboard or plywood

❷ Metal plate or tin lid to reinforce the entrance hole

❸ Metal hinge or strip of waterproof material

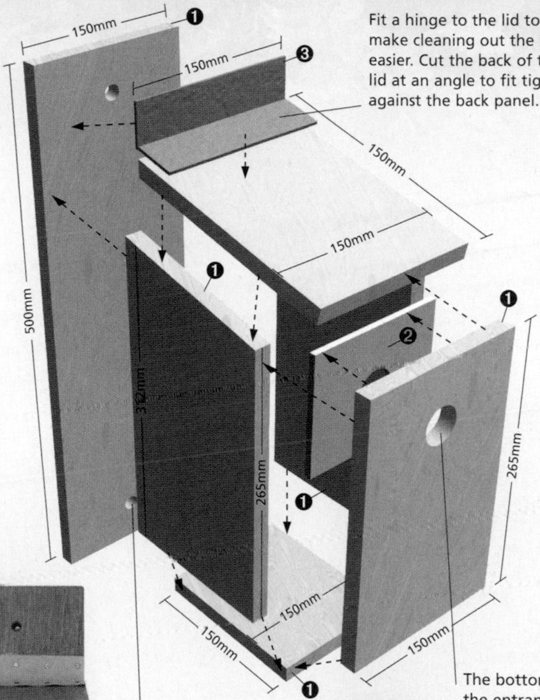

Fit a hinge to the lid to make cleaning out the box easier. Cut the back of the lid at an angle to fit tightly against the back panel.

150mm ❶
150mm ❸
150mm
150mm ❶
500mm
❶
150mm
265mm
❷
265mm
320mm
265mm
❶
150mm ❶
150mm
150mm ❶

Before assembly, drill a small attachment hole at the top and the bottom of the back panel

The bottom of the entrance hole must be at least 125mm from the floor of the box for the birds' safety

Completed nest box
Secure the box to a tree or wall using a screw at the top and another at the bottom. Add catches to the lid for extra security.

Convert to an open nest box
Replace the entrance hole panel with one that covers half of the front.

Threats to garden birds

Birds face many threats in the countryside, such as loss of habitat, mismanagement of the environment they depend upon, and natural and introduced predators. They are also in danger in gardens, but you can help to reduce the risks and make your garden a safe place for birds.

The importance of reducing threats

Some species of garden birds are in decline (see p.116 for the Big Garden Birdwatch results), and many factors – from unpredictable summers that affect breeding success to excessively "tidy" gardens – have had an impact on the numbers of several birds that were once common.

You can make a big difference not only by providing the right kind of natural and supplementary food for garden birds, but also by protecting their nesting sites and reducing the risk of predation. Natural predators will continue to prey on birds from healthy populations, but this is an inevitable part of the natural cycle.

Types of threats

Cats are a constant threat to garden birds. Where they are a menace, avoid leaving food on the ground and use a bird table that cats cannot reach. Place feeders at a height and away from places where they lurk. Make good use of spiny bushes at the base of feeders, and position nest boxes away from cats. You can also install electronic cat deterrents.

Sparrowhawks are a natural threat to smaller birds, but you should not discourage them from visiting your garden. They are a sign of a healthy environment and would not be around if bird populations

At a safe height
Remember to position nest boxes high above the ground to prevent cats from disturbing adult birds.

Nesting in house eaves
Do not discourage House Martins from building nests on your house. These migrants are a joy to be around.

Predator on the prowl
It is best to avoid placing nest boxes and feeders where cats have easy access. A bell on the collar can help warn birds.

were not high and sustainable. Moreover, they kill only for food, preying on the surplus population of weaker birds. However, you can protect garden birds from becoming easy prey by siting feeders carefully (see p.50).

Garden birds face threats from humans, too. Not cleaning feeders and bird tables regularly could lead to diseases in garden birds, which can then spread among populations.

Refer to the RSPB website for more information on this. Another threat comes from the use of pesticides, which can kill insects – vital food for birds.

Avoid cutting back, or removing, trees and hedges between March and August, which is the breeding time for birds. Encourage your neighbours to do maintenance outside this period. If you come to know of an active nest and suspect maintenance may occur, let those doing the work know. Cutting trees with active nests is a legal offence in the UK.

Say "no" to pesticides
Try not to use pesticides in your garden and let natural predators, including birds, do the job for you.

Small gardens

Size isn't everything when it comes to creating and maintaining a garden rich in habitat and food for birds. You can pack even the smallest of spaces with a range of features, providing a home for birds throughout the year.

Compact spaces

Make good use of small spaces in towns and cities by growing shrubs, climbers, and other plants up fences and walls. Use pots and hanging baskets to provide even more growing space

and mini "forests". Aim for structural diversity – add a shrub to provide good cover for birds, and include plants of a range of heights. Birds will soon take to feeders, and even nest boxes in quieter spots.

LAYOUT AND PLANTING IDEAS

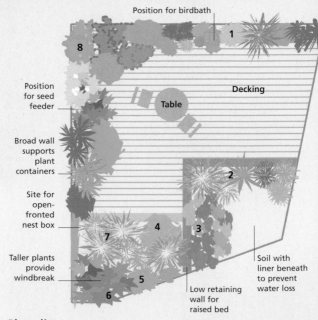

Position for birdbath
1

8

Position for seed feeder

Decking

Table

Broad wall supports plant containers

2

Site for open-fronted nest box

4

7

3

Taller plants provide windbreak

5

6

Soil with liner beneath to prevent water loss

Low retaining wall for raised bed

Plant list

1. **Herb Robert** *Geranium robertianum*
2. **Lavender** *Lavandula angustifolia*
3. **Common fumitory** *Fumaria officinalis*
4. **Thyme** *Thymus vulgaris*
5. **Red campion** *Silene dioica*
6. **Globe thistle** *Echinops ritro*
7. **Borage** *Borago officinalis*
8. **Lilac** *Syringa vulgaris*

Herb Robert
A wild relative of the geranium, Herb Robert grows well on walls and in rocky areas.

Lavender
This plant provides colour, scent, and seeds for birds. It is best to grow a mix of tall and short varieties.

Common fumitory
Growing well in bare areas, this plant produces many tubular red flowers that attract insects.

Thyme
This low-growing herb provides excellent ground cover. Its flowers draw insects in large numbers.

Red campion
When grown in pots and borders, this plant makes good cover. The big deep pink flowers attract insects.

Globe thistle
This tall plant is a good source of seeds. The blue flowers are a large draw for insects.

Borage
Well suited to small gardens, this blue-flowering herb thrives in dry, sunny spots.

Lilac
A richly scented shrub grown for cover, lilac can also be cut back to fit a smaller space.

Urban gardens

Urban areas are becoming increasingly important for birds. With the right planning, you can attract up to 20 species to any city garden. Provide as many habitats as you can for visitors at different times of the year.

Green haven

Think cover, places to feed, and water and you have the three key ingredients for attracting birds. A tree will provide perching places for birds coming into, and leaving, the garden. Fruiting and berry-bearing species provide autumn and winter food for them. Pack borders with nectar-rich plants for insects and seeds for birds in autumn and winter. Don't be too keen to cut these plants down – leave them to set seed.

LAYOUT AND PLANTING IDEAS

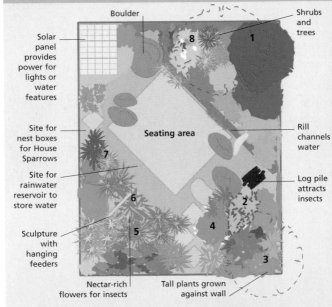

Boulder
Shrubs and trees
Solar panel provides power for lights or water features
8
1
Site for nest boxes for House Sparrows
Seating area
Rill channels water
7
Site for rainwater reservoir to store water
Log pile attracts insects
6
2
Sculpture with hanging feeders
4
5
3
Nectar-rich flowers for insects
Tall plants grown against wall

Plant list

1. **John Downie crab apple**
   Malus 'John Downie'

2. **Ox-eye daisy** *Leucanthemum vulgare*

3. **Sunflower** *Helianthus annuus*

4. **Stinging nettle** *Urtica dioica*

5. **Cornflower** *Centaurea cyanus*

6. **Ice plant** *Sedum spectabile*

7. **Red valerian** *Centranthus ruber*

8. **Bramble** *Rubus fruticosus*

John Downie crab apple
An ideal nesting site for wildlife, this tree attracts many insects and provides apples for thrushes.

Ox-eye daisy
The moderate height of this plant lends structure to a border. It also attracts insects to the garden.

Sunflower
This plant is a rich source of seeds for birds. Seeds can be collected and served up for birds later.

Stinging nettle
Butterflies including small tortoiseshell lay their eggs on this plant. It should be grown in a quiet corner.

Cornflower
A good fit in urban gardens, this medium-sized flower provides seeds for goldfinches in summer.

Ice plant
Best suited for borders, this low-growing plant attracts nectar-loving butterflies and bees.

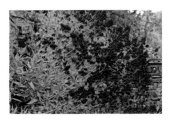

Red valerian
This plant adds a vivid splash of colour to borders and attracts insects to urban gardens.

Bramble
Providing cover and autumn fruit for birds, bramble needs pruning to prevent it from running too wild.

Suburban gardens

Being close to the countryside, many suburban gardens can link up with wildlife habitats used by birds, such as hedgerows. A good bird-friendly garden will form part of the territories of many birds and will be visited by several species.

On the outskirts

A good hedge is a key part of a well-maintained bird garden, providing cover and nesting sites. Privet gives year-round greenery, but aim for a useful "all-rounder" like hawthorn. Ivy is a must, giving food and shelter for birds. Make space for a pond, with native water plants, to provide water for birds and a home for aquatic wildlife. Leave a patch in your lawn to grow long, where wild plants such as violets can thrive.

LAYOUT AND PLANTING IDEAS

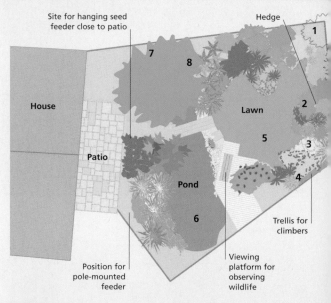

Site for hanging seed feeder close to patio

Hedge

House

Lawn

Patio

Pond

Trellis for climbers

Position for pole-mounted feeder

Viewing platform for observing wildlife

Plant list

1. **Rowan** Sorbus aucuparia
2. **Privet** Ligustrum vulgare
3. **Ivy** Hedera helix
4. **Honeysuckle** Lonicera periclymenum
5. **Sweet violet** Viola odorata

6. **Water violet or water plantain** Hottonia palustris or Alisma plantago-aquatica
7. **Holly** Ilex aquifolium
8. **Hawthorn** Crataegus monogyna

Rowan
If you have space for just one tree, rowan's superb crop of winter berries makes it the best choice.

Privet
This evergreen shrub gives year-long cover. The flowers, which bloom in summer, attract insects.

Ivy
Grown up a fence, ivy provides cover, nest sites, berries, and flowers for hoverflies, bees, and other insects.

Honeysuckle
This plant must be grown up against a wall or fence. Prune it to maintain bushy growth for birds to nest in.

Sweet violet
This plant is grown in lawns for colour and for providing nectar for insects.

Water violet and water plantain
Water violet and water plantain are perfect aquatic plants for a small-sized pond.

Holly
Providing year-round cover, holly makes a good nesting site. The red berries attract birds in autumn and winter.

Hawthorn
As well as shelter and nesting sites, this plant provides a feast of red berries for thrushes in autumn and winter.

Country gardens

You can make your own private nature reserve in a country garden by providing a wide range of habitats, scaling up features such as ponds, lawns, and flower borders, and by planting even more trees and shrubs.

Natural living

Provide ample cover with a native species hedge and at least two trees. Thick regrowth of some shrubs can be encouraged by coppicing – periodically cutting branches back to ground level. Make your pond as big as possible, keeping one end shallow to let birds drink and ensuring a good surface cover of water lilies. Pack borders with a range of plants that flower at different times of year, for instance, bugle blooms early in the year, foxgloves later.

LAYOUT AND PLANTING IDEAS

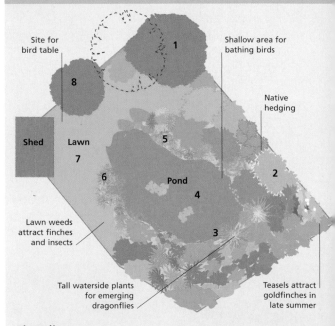

Site for bird table

Shallow area for bathing birds

Native hedging

Shed

Lawn

Lawn weeds attract finches and insects

Pond

Tall waterside plants for emerging dragonflies

Teasels attract goldfinches in late summer

Plant list

1. **Hazel** Corylus avellana
2. **Beech** Fagus sylvatica
3. **Purple loosestrife** Lythrum salicaria
4. **White water lily** Nymphaea alba
5. **Foxglove** Digitalis purpurea
6. **Cowslip** Primula veris
7. **Bugle** Ajuga reptans
8. **Bird cherry** Prunus padus

Hazel
Adding variety to a hedge or grown as a coppiced specimen, hazel produces pretty catkins in spring.

Beech
This plant provides a tall, thick hedge for roosting and nesting birds. The leaves stay on well into the winter.

Purple loosestrife
Grown at the edges of ponds for its rich purple hue, this tall plant provides perching places for birds.

White water lily
A must for a larger pond, this plant should be allowed to cover at least half of the water surface.

Foxglove
This robust, tall plant is suited for larger borders. The colourful flowers attract bees.

Cowslip
Elegant and low-growing, cowslip is a wildflower that brings early insects to the garden.

Bugle
Best grown in a larger lawn, bugle adds a pretty deep blue tinge to the garden. It attracts early insects.

Bird cherry
A good all-round wildlife tree, bird cherry provides excellent fruit for birds in autumn and winter.

How to identify

Watching a bird inevitably leads to asking "what is it?" Size, shape, plumage, behaviour, calls, and the season will point you to a bird's identity.

Anatomy

Becoming familiar with bird anatomy will hone your identification skills and give you an insight into how our feathered friends function. It will also add to your enjoyment when birdwatching.

Basics of bird anatomy

Birds are brilliantly built for flight, with a strong, lightweight skeleton, a covering of thousands of feathers of a variety of types, and strong muscles and wings. Having a lightweight beak instead of heavy teeth and jawbones also reduces their mass. Many bones in a bird's skeleton are hollow to make them

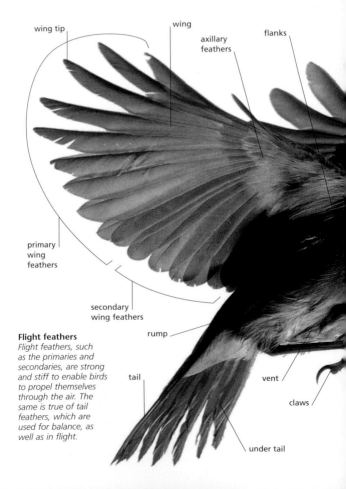

wing tip

wing

axillary feathers

flanks

primary wing feathers

secondary wing feathers

rump

Flight feathers
Flight feathers, such as the primaries and secondaries, are strong and stiff to enable birds to propel themselves through the air. The same is true of tail feathers, which are used for balance, as well as in flight.

tail

vent

claws

under tail

extra light. A honeycomb structure of struts within the bones adds the necessary strength.

Birds spend much of their time on the ground, and they must be agile on their feet. Garden birds need to be able to perch in trees and bushes, and therefore have strong, gripping feet and toes. Beaks come in numerous shapes and sizes, depending on the bird's diet and feeding style.

The eyes of most birds are on the sides of their head. This is called monocular vision, and its wide field of view allows birds to see any approaching danger quickly.

Feathers

Feathers serve a multitude of useful purposes for birds. They are used for heat conservation, waterproofing, camouflage, display, and flight. The image of the Robin shown here indicates some of the major feather types.

Feathers have a hollow shaft down the middle, with a flat area on each side – the vane. The bare base of the shaft is called the quill. The vane is made up of small side branches linked together by smaller hooked branches, called barbules.

Birds keep their feathers tidy and aerodynamic by "zipping up" the barbules using their beaks, which is why preening is such an important activity for birds.

eye

forehead

beak

chin

throat

breast

belly

feet

Contour feathers
The smaller, fluffy feathers on the body are called contour feathers. They lie flat and give birds their streamlined shape. The downy feathers that lie against the skin have excellent insulating properties.

BIRD SENSES
Owls have incredibly acute hearing and excellent vision. They can turn their heads through around 270°. Their disc-shaped faces are designed to trap and filter sound waves towards an owl's hidden ears. This process allows owls to detect the faint sound of mice and other prey. The Tawny Owl regularly visits gardens, although you are more likely to hear one calling at night than to see it.

Plumage and markings

A bird's feathers give a bird its colours and markings. The plumage of some birds is for display, while others are designed for camouflage. Males and females may have different plumages and markings, and young birds pose another identification challenge when they appear.

Changing appearances

The males and females of many species of birds are very similar, but in some cases, their appearances are strikingly different. Male and female Robins and Wrens are very hard to tell apart, but the different sexes of Blackbirds and Greenfinches are easy to identify.

Young birds also look very different to their parents. Their first set of feathers is known as juvenile plumage. As the autumn progresses, they attain first winter plumage. By this time, most young garden birds are virtually identical to adults.

Birds also change their appearance throughout the year. Some species have a distinct winter or non-breeding plumage. This is usually duller than breeding plumage. In spring, birds moult into a brand new set of feathers ready for the

Distinctive pattern
This Goldfinch is an easy bird to identify, with its striking red, black, and white face bands and golden wing bars.

FEATHER CARE
Birds must keep their plumage in excellent condition to retain their flying ability. Their daily grooming routine includes preening individual feathers with their beak using oil from a special preen gland on their back. This ensures the feathers remain waterproof. Old feathers are replaced one by one with new ones during a moult.

breeding season. By late summer, the adults' plumage is worn, so they perform another moult in the autumn, back into winter plumage.

Identifying feathers
As shown here, the individual feathers of birds are very different. With practise you may be able to identify some of the feathers you find in your garden.

and above the eye, wing bars, the pattern of the head, tail bands, and rump patches. The upper and underparts are often different colours and the latter may be strongly marked, as with the speckling on thrushes.

STARLING   **JAY**

BLACKBIRD

TAWNY OWL

Markings

Many birds have a rich array of different markings in their plumage from stripes and spots to bars and chevrons. Look carefully at the exact position of these markings on the bird as an aid to identification. Some key areas to look for are stripes through

Male siskin markings
This male Siskin may be small, but it is beautifully marked. Its plumage is an intricate mix of black, yellow, and green.

Black cap

Yellow bar on wings

Dark streaks on green back

Yellow patch on tail

Size and shape

Garden birds come in an array of shapes and sizes. Familiarizing yourself with the body types of the major garden bird groups is a great start.

Size

When faced with an unfamiliar bird, compare its size with a bird you know well, such as a Blackbird. See if it is smaller, larger, or about the same size. You can also use the size of objects in the garden to help you get an idea of its size.

Young birds may take a while to reach full adult size, and there may be a difference in size between sexes, as with the Sparrowhawk.

Remember that birds fluff up their feathers in cold weather to look bigger, and may appear smaller and sleeker after a bath.

Compare and contrast
Compare the size and shape of mystery birds to common species such as Blackbirds and Blue Tits (below) to help you with identification.

Classic shape
A Robin's plump breast and upright stance make it instantly recognizable, even when its red breast is obscured.

Shape

Each species of bird also has a distinctive shape, with factors such as posture, leg and beak length, and the way it behaves all providing additional information. These clues help you assign a bird to a particular family and narrow down the possibilities when consulting an identification guide.

For example, thrushes are slender and upright, pigeons and doves are plump and small-headed, and tits are small and compact. As with size, it is helpful to compare the shape of a mystery bird with a familiar species. Is it chunkier than a Greenfinch, say, or more slender than a Robin?

Neighbourhood watch
Watch your garden birds regularly and you will get to know their behaviour and body types. Compare them with one another to help with identification.

Small head
Round body
Crouching stance

DUNNOCK

Stocky build
Long tail

HOUSE SPARROW

Small, round head
Plump breast

Small, flat head
Sharply pointed wings
Shallow, forked tail

SWIFT

Round-tipped tail

COLLARED DOVE

Beak and tail shape

There are clues to a bird's identity in its beak and tail shape, so make sure you always look at the front and back ends of the birds you see. Garden birds have a number of different beak shapes depending on what they eat, and display a range of different lengths and shapes of tail.

Beak shape

As you spend time observing birds in your garden and watching them feed, the variety of beak styles will become apparent. With practice, you will be able to identify finches and sparrows from their strong, stubby beaks, tits from their small, short beaks, and warblers by their slender beaks.

These subtle differences can be very useful for identification purposes. A bird's beak can give you many clues as to what it eats,

Balancing act
The Long-tailed Tit's long, narrow tail trails out behind it in flight and helps with balance in trees and bushes. Its tiny beak is designed for eating insects.

and thus which family of birds it belongs to. You should also watch how birds use their beaks. You won't see a Spotted Flycatcher probing its slender insect-catching beak into your lawn because it is an aerial feeder, but Starlings probe their long, slender beaks into the grass like sewing machines.

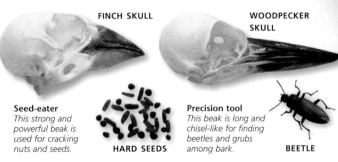

FINCH SKULL

WOODPECKER SKULL

Seed-eater
This strong and powerful beak is used for cracking nuts and seeds.

HARD SEEDS

Precision tool
This beak is long and chisel-like for finding beetles and grubs among bark.

BEETLE

THRUSH SKULL

TAWNY OWL SKULL

Multi-purpose beak
This beak can tackle fruit and all kinds of invertebrates, from worms to snails.

SNAIL SHELL

Meat-eater
This sharp beak has a hooked tip for seizing small mammals and tearing flesh.

MEAT STRIP

Tail shape

Take away the bold black and white colours on a Magpie and its extra-long tail would be its most eye-catching feature. Many garden birds have distinctive tails, so it is always worth trying to ascertain their size and shape.

Look at the very end to see if it is round-tipped, straight-tipped, forked, or adorned with streamers, as with the Swallow. Some birds hold their tails in distinctive ways. Wrens cock theirs and Collared Doves fan theirs as they soar round in display flight.

Feeding the family
The Robin's fine beak shows it is mainly an insect eater. Here, it is packed with insects for its brood.

Wing shape

Many of your sightings of birds will be when they are doing what they do best – flying. Birds have various flight styles, and the more time you spend watching them, the clearer the differences will be. From rapid wingbeats to graceful gliding, each style is unique and a joy to watch.

Wing types

Every bird's wings are made to suit its lifestyle. Swifts spend most of their lives in flight, so they have long, pointed wings to enable them to glide through the air with ease. Migrant birds have long wings in relation to their body, as they have to fly thousands of miles every year. Resident birds such as Wrens and tits have very short wings, as they cover long distances by hopping through bushes and trees.

Seeing a bird in flight is the best way to view its wing type. Check the wingtips – are they sharply pointed or round? You can also get an idea of wing length when you see it perched. Look to see where the wings end in relation to the tail.

Agile flight
Greenfinches have long wings and a dashing, agile flight. In this photograph, one individual is passing food to another.

Flight control

Some birds, such as Swifts and Sparrowhawks, are built for speed, while others, for example Tawny Owls, are built for a silent, stealthy flight in order to surprise their prey. Smaller birds have to beat their wings rapidly to fly, but other larger birds are able to spread their broad wings and use rising pockets of air, called thermals, to glide across the sky with minimum effort. You may see Black-headed Gulls, Rooks, and Jackdaws soaring around over your garden from time to time on hot days. A few birds, including Kestrels, can hover in midair.

Taking wing
Garden birds display a wide range of wing shapes and flight styles, which will become apparent as you observe them.

Rounded wings
Blue tits have short, round wings, which are typical of a bird that doesn't have to fly far.

Pointed wings
Starlings have pointed wings, which gives them an arrow shape in flight. They are amazingly agile in large roosts.

Rapid flight
The Feral Pigeon is a descendent of racing pigeons, so it has pointed wings ideal for fast flight.

WOODPECKER WINGS

Woodpeckers spend most of their lives in the treetops and rarely have to fly over long distances. They have short, round wings, which they beat quickly and then glide for a time, giving them a striking undulating flight pattern. This style of flight enables them to be recognized even from far away.

Green Woodpecker wing
Woodpeckers' wings help the birds to balance as they clamber around trees.

Watching

Watching garden birds is entertaining and educational. If you have followed some of the advice in the previous pages about attracting birds to your garden, you will be treated to a regular display of avian activity.

Basic tools

Having made the effort to attract birds to your garden, you will want to be able to reap the benefits. Get good views of the birds in your garden and make sure you don't miss any exciting visitors or fascinating bits of behaviour.

One of the joys of watching birds is that it costs nothing and is easy to do. Anyone, regardless of age or bird expertise, can become a birdwatcher. All you need to enjoy the birds in your garden is your eyes and ears, and some time to devote to watching them.

It is well worth considering investing in a pair of binoculars. This will bring the birds close-up, and help with their identification.

Shy visitor
Views of exciting birds like this Great Spotted Woodpecker are thrilling. This species can be shy, so avoid sudden movements if one visits your feeder.

When to watch

Early morning is a time of great activity for birds with peak feeding, singing, and courtship activity and many birds present. It is well worth getting up early to watch this surge in activity.

Late afternoon provides another peak of activity. Birds prepare for the night with a feeding frenzy and you may see birds going to roost. Flocks of Starlings stream over in autumn and winter, and Swifts spiral into the sky to roost on the wing in summer.

Natural camouflage
Use natural cover, such as trees, to help break up your outline if you are watching birds outdoors.

Getting the best view

Hopefully, you will have already put careful thought into where you have positioned your feeders, bird tables, and nest boxes so that you have a clear view.

If you are watching from inside, through a window, you have the perfect hide as birds will not be able to see your outline. Try to keep noise to a minimum and avoid sudden movements.

The longer a feeder or bird table has been in position, the more comfortable birds will feel using it. They will also become more used to your presence, giving you even better views as they feed.

BIRD SURVEY

As you spend time watching the birds in your garden, you may find you want to keep a record of how many birds are visiting. You will notice differences in numbers at various times of the day, throughout the year, and from year to year, raising all sorts of fascinating questions.

Counting the birds
A clicker is the perfect way to keep a count of the birds in your garden – great for keeping score for the RSPB's Big Garden Birdwatch.

Bird behaviour

The way birds behave varies with species, age and sex, time of year, time of day, and even the weather. By watching regularly, you will get an insight into a wide variety of interactions both among different species and between individuals of the same species.

Night-time watching
Watching doesn't have to stop at night, which is when Tawny Owls usually visit gardens with mature trees.

Recognizing individuals
Some birds can be recognized individually by their behaviour. Some others, such as this albino Blackbird, can be identified by distinctive markings.

Feeding is probably the easiest behaviour to watch in your garden birds – whether they are coming in to feed on the supplementary food you provide or on natural food such as insects, berries, and seeds. You will see more birds in cold weather, when food is scarce in other gardens and the countryside.

One of the most interesting behaviours to look out for is courtship and territorial disputes. Courtship includes the singing of the male birds and displays such as the aerial, "bat-like" pirouettes performed by male Greenfinches and the blink-and-you-miss-it parties of "screaming" Swifts racing around overhead and through your garden in summer. Courtship also involves mutual preening (grooming of feathers), as well as male birds presenting food to females. Look out for the way birds interact and work as a team in flocks. When young birds are in the nest, you will also be able to observe the complete devotion of adults to their offspring.

Care of the young
Some species, including Swallows, can raise three broods in summer if the weather is good.

Watching through the year

You can spot the best variety and the most number of birds in your garden in winter. During this time, birds focus on finding enough food to maintain their fat reserves and energy levels to survive the cold nights. Winter is also the time to spot flocks of Starlings, Lesser Redpolls, Siskins, and many others.

down with a mate, build a nest (some species build more than one), and get on with breeding.

May is the first month when the young of resident garden birds can be seen in large numbers. Some species can raise three broods in a year, but this depends on the weather.

Many garden birds may leave in autumn to take advantage of the

Changing feathers
In winter, Starling plumage is white-spotted in contrast to the plainer, glossy breeding plumage.

As winter turns to spring, the sound of birdsong makes a welcome return. Some winter-visiting birds "tune up" before leaving, but residents are keen to get on, with Song Thrushes and Blackbirds being among the earliest to be heard. Once territories are established, it's time to attract, select, and settle

bounty the countryside has to offer, but they will return. In autumn, birds that are migrating south may start to arrive in your garden, providing an opportunity to see some unusual species. Chances are you may spot a Redstart, Pied or Spotted Flycatcher, or Firecrest.

Returning visitors
Migrant House Martins come back to their breeding territories in houses between the second half of April and early May.

Bird profiles

KEY TO SYMBOLS

♀ female   ♂ male

☾ juvenile   ☺ immature
● adult

❦ spring   ☼ summer
🍂 autumn   ❄ winter

DISTRIBUTION MAPS

Each species profile includes a map showing the range of the species, with colours reflecting seasonal location.

SCALE INDICATORS

Each species is compared to one of four well-know birds, for an accurate indication of size.

Mute Swan   Mallard   Feral Pigeon   House Sparrow

■ Summer distribution

■ Resident all year

■ Seen on migration

■ Winter distribution

Grey Heron

Ardea cinerea

Standing still as a statue or walking slowly through the shallows before suddenly straightening its neck with lightning speed to seize a fish in its powerful bill, this big, grey heron is easy to identify. It may also be slimmer or hunched, and can perch in a tree or perform dramatic aerobatics.

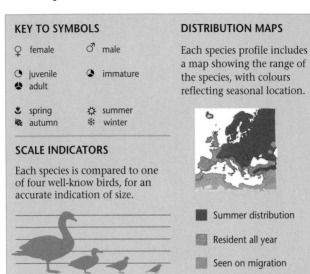

dagger-like yellowish bill; orange in spring

FEEDS IN *fresh and salt water habitats, from estuaries to garden ponds in urban areas.*

head with grey cap; lacks crest

grey sides of head and neck

wispy black plume

pale grey body

broad, bowed, grey and black wings

black streaks on white foreneck

long yellowish legs, reddish in spring

VOICE *Loud, harsh fraink; squawking, croaking, and bill-snapping at nest.*
NESTING *Large nest of stout sticks, usually in treetop colony; 4–5 eggs; 1 brood; Jan–May.*
FEEDING *Seizes fish, frogs, small mammals, and other prey in its bill, typically after long, patient stalk before sudden strike.*
SIMILAR SPECIES *Purple Heron.*

Sparrowhawk

Accipiter nisus

HUNTS IN *wide variety of habitats, from dense forests to cities. Breeds in wooded farmland and forest; winters in more open country.*

The Sparrowhawk is a small, quick, agile bird hunter, adapted for pursuing its prey through forests. It has relatively short, broad wings and a long tail, giving it great manoeuvrability. It often dashes into view at low level with a distinctive flap-flap-glide action, then jinks and swerves to disappear through a tight gap. At other times, it soars over the woods on fanned wings, sweeping them back to a point in fast glides. The male, much smaller than the female, is blue-grey above with bright rusty orange below; the female is browner above and whitish barred with grey below.

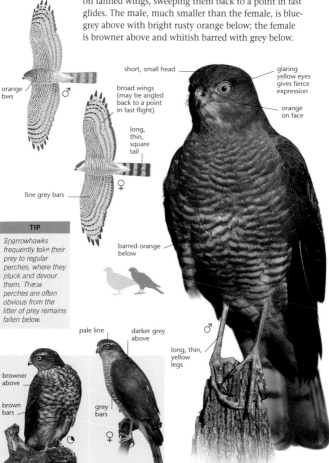

orange bws ♂

short, small head

broad wings (may be angled back to a point in fast flight)

long, thin, square tail ♀

fine grey bars

glaring yellow eyes gives fierce expression

orange on face

barred orange below

pale line

darker grey above

browner above

brown bars

grey bars ♀

♂

long, thin, yellow legs

TIP

Sparrowhawks frequently take their prey to regular perches, where they pluck and devour them. These perches are often obvious from the litter of prey remains fallen below.

VOICE *Repetitive* kek-kek-kek-kek-kek, *thin squealing* peee-ee, *but generally quiet away from nest.*
NESTING *Small, flat platform of thin twigs on flat branch close to tree trunk; 4–5 eggs; 1 brood; Mar–Jun.*
FEEDING *Hunts small birds, darting along hedges, woodland edges, or into gardens to take prey by surprise; males take mainly tits and finches, larger females take thrushes and pigeons.*
SIMILAR SPECIES *Kestrel, Goshawk.*

Rock Dove

Columba livia

The wild ancestor of the town or feral pigeon, the Rock Dove is a bird of rocky coasts and crags. It is paler, with an ash-grey back, a green and purple gloss on its neck, two broad black wingbars, and a white rump. Feral pigeons have very varied plumage patterns, and interbreeding between the two forms has made the genuine wild Rock Dove a rarity.

BREEDS ON *coastal cliffs and mountains. Feral birds widespread from coasts to cities, and on farmland.*

tiny white patch

pale grey back

larger white patch

glossy purple and green on neck

FERAL PIGEON

dark below

white rump

white underwing

two long, broad, black bars on wings

VOICE *Deep, rolling, moaning* coo, oo-ooh-oorr, oo-roo-coo.
NESTING *Loose, untidy, sparse nest on ledge or in cavity; 2 eggs; 3 broods; all year.*
FEEDING *Forages for seeds, buds, berries, and small invertebrates on ground.*
SIMILAR SPECIES *Woodpigeon, Stock Dove, Peregrine or other birds of prey in flight.*

Woodpigeon

Columba palumbus

A large, common, boldly marked pigeon, often found in large flocks, the Woodpigeon is usually identifiable by its white neck patch, pink breast, white wingbar, and plump, small-headed look. Although tame in city parks, it is shy in rural areas where it is persecuted as a pest.

FEEDS MAINLY *on farmland; breeds in a variety of woodland and farmland with trees, also town parks and big gardens.*

rump paler than back

bold white neck patch

grey back

dark tail band

large white midwing patch

pink breast

dull red legs

white on wings

no white on neck

duller

broad dark band at end of tail

VOICE *Husky, muffled, repeated cooing,* coo-coo-cu, cu-coo, cook; *loud wing clatter in sudden take-off; wing claps in display flight.*
NESTING *Thin platform of twigs in tree or bush; 2 eggs; 1–2 broods; Apr–Sep.*
FEEDING *Eats, buds, leaves, berries, and fruit in trees and on ground; visits bird tables.*
SIMILAR SPECIES *Stock Dove, Rock Dove.*

Collared Dove

Streptopelia decaocto

LIVES IN *woodlands, parks, gardens, around farm buildings, and in villages and towns.*

Identifiable by its pale, grey-brown body, its thin, black half-collar, and monotonous triple coo, the Collared Dove is common on farms and in suburbs. It prefers to nest and roost in tall conifers. The male has a dramatic display flight, rising steeply and gliding down in wide arcs on flat wings, with harsh nasal calls.

grey area on upperwings

dark wingtips

white-tipped tail

pale, grey-brown body

black half-collar

pinkish head and breast

no collar

sandy-buff

VOICE *Loud, repeated triple cu-cooo-cuk; also a nasal gwurrrr call in flight.*
NESTING *Small platform of twigs, rubbish; 2 eggs; 2–3 broods (or more); all year.*
FEEDING *Picks grain, seeds, and shoots from ground; often takes seeds from bird tables.*
SIMILAR SPECIES *Turtle Dove, Rock Dove, Kestrel.*

Tawny Owl

Strix aluco

HUNTS IN *all kinds of woodland, wooded farmland, and also in urban parks and large gardens with trees, even in big cities.*

A big-headed, bulky woodland owl that is generally strictly nocturnal, the Tawny Owl is responsible for the hooting and loud *ke-wick* notes often heard after dark. Beautifully camouflaged, it is hard to spot while roosting in the trees unless betrayed by the mobbing of small birds.

large black eyes

obvious facial disc

large, round head

brown back with row of white spots on each side

short wings and tail

pale spots and bars

VOICE *Loud, excited, yapping ke-wick!, long, quavering hoot, hoo hoo-hooo hoo-o-o.*
NESTING *Hole in tree or building, or old stick nest of crow; 2–5 eggs; 1 brood; Apr–Jun.*
FEEDING *Drops down to take rodents, frogs, beetles, and worms; also small roosting birds.*
SIMILAR SPECIES *Long-eared Owl, Eagle Owl, Tengmalm's Owl.*

Green Woodpecker

Picus viridis

LIVES IN *and around broadleaved and mixed woodland, and heathy places with bushes and trees. Feeds on grassy areas with ants.*

Easily detected, especially in spring, by its loud laughing calls, this big, pale woodpecker forages mainly on the ground. A wary feeder, it is often spotted as it flies up and into cover. Adults are mainly bright green with crimson crowns; young birds are mottled.

red and black moustache; no red in female

black around whitish eye

bright greenish yellow rump

vivid red cap (in both sexes)

blackish spots and streaks

dark wingtips with pale bars

apple-green upperside

greenish yellow rump

VOICE *Loud, shrill, bouncing keu-keu-keuk; song a descending kleu-kleu-kleu-keu-keu.*
NESTING *Bores nest hole in tree; 5–7 eggs; 1 brood; May–Jul.*
FEEDING *Eats ants, ants' eggs, and larvae, mainly on ground, using long, sticky tongue to probe nests.*
SIMILAR SPECIES *Golden Oriole.*

Great Spotted Woodpecker

Dendrocopos major

The rapid "drum roll" of this bird is a common sound of spring wood-land. The woodpecker itself is often easy to locate, propped on its tail as it hammers at bark or timber. Although similar to the Middle Spotted, it has less red on its head, and more beneath its tail.

red patch on back of head

FEEDS IN *gardens and scrub as well as mature woodland; breeds in both deciduous and conifer woods.*

bold black and white above

bright buff below

all-red crown; less on female

big white shoulder patch

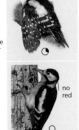

no red

vivid red under tail

VOICE *Explosive tchik! fast rattle of alarm; loud, fast, very short drumming.*
NESTING *Bores nest hole in tree trunk or branch; 4–7 eggs; 1 brood; Apr–Jun.*
FEEDING *Digs insects and grubs from bark with strong bill; also eats seeds and berries.*
SIMILAR SPECIES *Middle Spotted Woodpecker, Lesser Spotted Woodpecker.*

Pied Wagtail

Motacilla alba

Common throughout Europe, this boldly patterned wagtail occurs in two forms. The darker Pied Wagtail of Britain and Ireland has a black back, dark flanks, and blackish wings, and the White Wagtail of mainland Europe (which also occurs as a passage migrant in spring and autumn in the British Isles) has a pale grey back and rump, and pale flanks. Both occur in a wide variety of habitats, from farmland to urban areas. They chase insects with agile leaps and runs, constantly nodding their heads and bobbing their long tails.

ROOSTS INCLUDE *trees in town centres; the birds feed in car parks, roadsides, and rooftops; also in farmyards, fields, often by water.*

black cap, chin, and throat; white chin and throat in winter

whitish face

blackish rump

♂ ☼

white streaks on wings

black breast

black back

sooty flanks

white feather edges

greyer back

white below

♀ PIED

white belly

greyer above

buffish below

♂ ☼ PIED

long black tail with white edges

♂ WHITE WAGTAIL
M.a.alba

pale grey back and rump

black tail, same as Pied form

TIP

Outside the breeding season Pied and White Wagtails form communal roosts, often with hundreds of birds. These roosts may occur in natural sites such as small trees or reedbeds, but in some areas wagtail roosts can be found on buildings, or even inside large commercial glasshouses, where the birds perch in long lines on the steel cross-beams below the roof.

VOICE *Call loud, musical* chirp, chuwee, chrruwee, *grading into harder* tissik *or* chiswik; *song mixture of these calls and trills.*
NESTING *Grassy cup in cavity in bank, wall, cliff, or woodpile, in outbuilding or under bridge; 5–6 eggs; 2–3 broods; Apr–Aug.*
FEEDING *Feeds very actively on ground, roofs, or waterside mud or rocks, walking, running, leaping up or sideways, or flying in pursuit of flies; also takes other insects, molluscs, and some seeds.*
SIMILAR SPECIES *Grey Wagtail, juvenile Yellow Wagtail.*

Wren

Troglodytes troglodytes

SINGS FROM *exposed perches, but more often seen foraging in thick cover at low level, in woods and thickets.*

A tiny, plump, finely-barred bird with a surprisingly loud voice, the Wren has a habit of raising its very short tail vertically. It also has a distinctive flight: fast and direct, often plunging straight into dense cover. Wren populations decline in cold winters, but usually recover quite quickly.

very slightly downcurved, fine bill

pale stripe over eye

dark barring

short, rounded tail

rusty-brown above with barred wings

faint bars

strong legs and feet

VOICE *Hard, rattling chit, chiti, tzerr; song amazingly loud, fast, warbling with low trill.*
NESTING *Small, loose ball of leaves and grass in bank; 5–6 eggs; 2 broods; Apr–Jul.*
FEEDING *Forages for insects and spiders in low, thick cover, under hedges, in ditches, and other dark, damp places.*
SIMILAR SPECIES *Dunnock, Robin.*

Dunnock

Prunella modularis

FORAGES FOR *food in low, dense scrub and bushes, on heaths and moors, and in forests, woods, parks, and gardens.*

Although it is one of many small, streaky, sparrow-like birds, the Dunnock has a fine bill, grey head and breast, and forages on the ground with a distinctive, jerky, creeping shuffle. If disturbed, it generally flies at ground level into the nearest thick bush.

red-brown eyes

fine, dark bill

grey throat

pale spots on wings

browner head

rich brown with black streaks

orange-brown legs

black-streaked brown wings and back

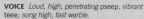

VOICE *Loud, high, penetrating pseep, vibrant teee; song high, fast warble.*
NESTING *Small grassy cup lined with hair, moss, in bush; 4–5 eggs; 2–3 broods; Apr–Jul.*
FEEDING *Picks small insects and seeds from ground, shuffling under and around bushes.*
SIMILAR SPECIES *Robin, Wren, House Sparrow.*

Robin

Erithacus rubecula

The round-bodied, slim-tailed Robin is a shy, skulking woodland bird over most of its range. It is adapted for following animals such as wild boar and taking small animals from the earth they disturb. In the UK, it follows gardeners instead, and has become very tame.

LIVES IN *open forests and woods, on bushy heaths, and in parks and gardens with hedges and shrubs.*

big black eye

orange-red breast

bluish grey on sides of neck and chest

warm brown above

white breast spot

mottled brown body

VOICE *Sharp* tik, *quick* tik-ik-ik-ik, *high, thin* seep; *song rich, sweet, musical, varied warble.*
NESTING *Domed nest of leaves and grass in bank or bush; 4–6 eggs; 2 broods; Apr–Aug.*
FEEDING *Takes spiders, insects, worms, berries, and seeds, mostly from ground.*
SIMILAR SPECIES *Dunnock, Nightingale, Redstart.*

Blackbird

Turdus merula

A smart, plump thrush with a distinctive habit of raising its tail on landing, the Blackbird is a familiar garden bird. The glossy black male is easy to recognize, but the brown female can be confused with other thrushes despite her darker plumage. Males sing superbly, especially from high perches towards dusk.

LIVES IN *woods with leaf litter, also parks and gardens, and farmland with tall hedges.*

yellow bill and eye-ring

paler wingtips

all-black body

dark brown legs

♂

gingery body

dark bill

dull black
♂ 1ST

dark brown

mottled below

♀

VOICE *Low, soft* chook, *frequent* pink-pink-pink, *fast alarm rattle, high* srreee; *song superb, musical, varied, full-throated warbling.*
NESTING *Grass and mud cup in shrub or low in tree; 3–5 eggs; 2–4 broods; Mar–Aug.*
FEEDING *Finds worms, insects, and spiders on ground; fruit and berries in bushes.*
SIMILAR SPECIES *Ring Ouzel, Song Thrush.*

Fieldfare

Turdus pilaris

A large, handsome thrush with a striking combination of
plumage colours, the Fieldfare is usually identifiable by its
blue-grey head and white underwing. It is a winter visitor to
most of Europe, like the smaller Redwing, and the two often
feed together in mixed flocks, stripping berries
from fruiting trees and shrubs.

FEEDS ON *farmland,
bushy heaths, woods,
orchards, and gardens
in winter; breeds
in woodland.*

blue-grey head
with black mask

black and
yellow bill

white
under-
wings

dark brown
back

orange-buff breast
with heavy black spots

pale
grey rump

black
tail

whiter
flanks

dense black
chevrons on
white flanks

VOICE Loud, chuckling chak-chak-chak, low,
nasal weeip; song a rather unmusical mixture
of squeaks, warbles, and whistles.
NESTING Cup of grass and twigs in bush or
tree; 5–6 eggs; 1–2 broods; May–Jun.
FEEDING Mostly eats worms and insects on
the ground; also fruit from trees and bushes.
SIMILAR SPECIES Mistle Thrush, Blackbird.

Mistle Thrush

Turdus viscivorus

Big, bold, and aggressive, the Mistle Thrush is
the largest of the European thrushes. It has
a tall, long-necked look compared to the
Song Thrush, and often flies much
higher when disturbed. Males often
sing from the tops of tall trees in all
weathers, and in winter
single birds defend
berry-laden trees
against Fieldfares,
Redwings, and
other birds.

bold dark
eye

BREEDS ON *farmland
with tall trees, edges of
moorland near forest,
woodland clearings,
orchards, and parks.*

slender
neck

grey-brown
back

pale outer
coverts

white
underwings

pale
rump

bold black spots
on creamy buff
underside

whitish tail
sides

pale head

pale
spots

VOICE Loud, rattling chatter, tsairrk-sairr-
sairr-sairk; song repeated wild, fluty phrases.
NESTING Loose cup of twigs and grass high
in tree; 3–5 eggs; 2 broods; Mar–Jun.
FEEDING Hops on ground, taking seeds and
invertebrates; also eats berries and fruits.
SIMILAR SPECIES Song Thrush, Fieldfare,
female Blackbird.

Song Thrush

Turdus philomelos

Small, pale, and neatly spotted below, the Song Thrush is a familiar bird with a wonderfully vibrant, varied, full-throated song. Well-known for its habit of smashing the shells of snails to extract their soft bodies, it also hauls many earthworms from their burrows. It is declining in many areas, particularly on farmland.

BREEDS AND *feeds in broadleaved woodland, farmland with trees and hedges, parks and gardens with shrubs.*

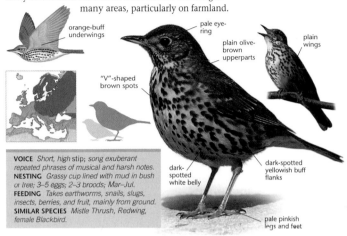

orange-buff underwings

pale eye-ring

plain olive-brown upperparts

plain wings

"V"-shaped brown spots

dark-spotted white belly

dark-spotted yellowish buff flanks

pale pinkish legs and feet

VOICE *Short, high stip; song exuberant repeated phrases of musical and harsh notes.*
NESTING *Grassy cup lined with mud in bush or tree; 3–5 eggs; 2–3 broods; Mar–Jul.*
FEEDING *Takes earthworms, snails, slugs, insects, berries, and fruit, mainly from ground.*
SIMILAR SPECIES *Mistle Thrush, Redwing, female Blackbird.*

Redwing

Turdus iliacus

A small, sociable thrush with a bold head pattern and well-defined streaks below, the Redwing is named for its distinctive rusty-red underwings and flanks. It is a winter visitor to much of Europe from the taiga forests of the far north, and typically forages in flocks for berries, often with Fieldfares. In hard winters, it often visits large gardens for food.

FEEDS IN *winter flocks on farmland with hedges, bushy heaths, and gardens.*

dark cap

reddish underwing

bold pale stripe over eye

dark brown back

pale stripe under dark cheeks

short, square tail

dull rust-red flanks

silvery white below, with dark streaks

TIP

On calm, clear autumn nights, migrant Redwings can often be heard flying overhead, calling to each other to stay in contact.

VOICE *Flight call thin, high seeeh, also chuk, chittuk; song variable repetition of short phrases and chuckling notes.*
NESTING *Cup of grass and twigs, in low bush; 4–6 eggs; 2 broods; Apr–Jul.*
FEEDING *Worms, insects, and seeds taken from ground in winter.*
SIMILAR SPECIES *Song Thrush, Skylark.*

Blackcap

Sylvia atricapilla

The Blackcap is a stocky warbler with a typical, hard, unmusical call. Its song, however, is beautiful, rich, and full-throated, less even than the similar song of the Garden Warbler. It may overwinter in northwest Europe, when it visits gardens to take seeds and scraps, often driving other birds away from feeders.

SINGS *brilliantly from perches in woods, parks, and large bushy gardens, with plenty of thick undergrowth.*

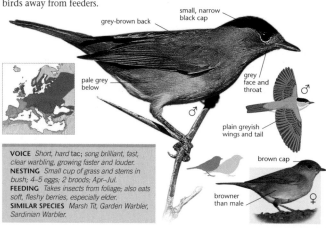

small, narrow black cap

grey-brown back

pale grey below

♂

grey face and throat

plain greyish wings and tail

brown cap

browner than male

♀

VOICE *Short, hard tac; song brilliant, fast, clear warbling, growing faster and louder.*
NESTING *Small cup of grass and stems in bush; 4–5 eggs; 2 broods; Apr–Jul.*
FEEDING *Takes insects from foliage; also eats soft, fleshy berries, especially elder.*
SIMILAR SPECIES *Marsh Tit, Garden Warbler, Sardinian Warbler.*

Chiffchaff

Phylloscopus collybita

By sight the Chiffchaff is almost impossible to distinguish from the Willow Warbler, although the slightly plumper Chiffchaff's habit of dipping its tail downward is a useful clue. When it sings, it betrays its identity by repeating its name over and over again – and luckily it sings a lot, particularly in spring. Some Chiffchaffs spend the winter in western Europe, unlike Willow Warblers.

REPEATS ITS *name from perches in woodland, parks, bushy areas, and large gardens; favours taller trees in summer.*

short, round wings

rounder head than Willow Warbler

white crescent under eye

dips tail while feeding

blackish legs

olive body

VOICE *Call slurred, sweet hweet; song easy, bright chip-chap-chip-chap-chip-chup-chip.*
NESTING *Domed grass nest, low in bush or undergrowth; 5–6 eggs; 1–2 broods; Apr–Jul.*
FEEDING *Takes insects and spiders from leaves, slipping easily through foliage.*
SIMILAR SPECIES *Willow Warbler, Wood Warbler.*

Goldcrest

Regulus regulus

Europe's smallest bird, the agile, busy Goldcrest frequently forages very close to people, apparently oblivious of their presence. This needle-billed, round-bodied bird often gives its high-pitched calls as it searches restlessly for food. It has a plainer face than its close relative, the Firecrest.

FEEDS IN *coniferous and mixed woodland, thickets, and large gardens, throughout the year.*

broad white "V"

olive-green back

blackish wings

yellow inner stripe on black crown

buff below

VOICE High, sibilant see-see-see call; high, fast song, seedli-ee seedli-ee seedli-ee.
NESTING Cup of cobwebs and moss, slung from branch; 7–8 eggs; 2 broods; Apr–Jul.
FEEDING Picks tiny insects, spiders, and insect eggs from foliage, often hovering briefly.
SIMILAR SPECIES Firecrest, Willow Warbler, Chiffchaff.

Long-tailed Tit

Aegithalos caudatus

The tiny rounded body and slender tail of the Long-tailed Tit give it a ball-and-stick shape that is quite unique among European birds. In summer, family parties move noisily through bushes and undergrowth, but in winter they often travel through woodland in much larger groups, crossing gaps between the trees, one or two at a time.

LIVES IN *woods with bushy undergrowth. Increasingly visits garden feeders.*

black and pink back

black band on white head; all-white in N. race

pink shoulders

long, black, white-sided tail

black and white plumage

dark wings

dull white below

VOICE High, thin, colourless seee seee seee; short, abrupt, low trrp or zerrp.
NESTING Rounded nest of lichen, moss, cobwebs, and feathers with side entrance, in low bush; 8–12 eggs; 1 brood; Apr–Jun.
FEEDING Tiny insects and spiders taken from twigs and foliage; some seeds.
SIMILAR SPECIES None.

Marsh Tit

Parus palustris

Virtually identical to the Willow Tit in its appearance, the slightly slimmer, neater Marsh Tit is most easily identified by its distinctive *pit-chew* call. Despite its name, it is not found in marshes, but prefers mature broadleaved woodland where it often feeds at low level among thick undergrowth.

glossy black cap and back of neck

FORAGES AMONG *tall deciduous trees in woodland and parks, especially beech and oak; also in gardens.*

black bib, smaller than Willow Tit's

neck slimmer than Willow Tit's

pale grey-buff underside

neat, plain grey-brown upperparts

rounded grey-brown wings

VOICE *Bright* pit-chew! *and* titi-zee-zee-zee; *song rippling* schip-schip-schip-schip.
NESTING *Grass and moss cup in pre-existing tree hole; 6–8 eggs, 1 brood; Apr–Jun.*
FEEDING *Mostly insects and spiders in summer; seeds, berries, and nuts in winter.*
SIMILAR SPECIES *Willow Tit, Coal Tit, Blackcap.*

Coal tit

Parus ater

FORAGES AMONG *pines and other conifers; also feeds in low shrubs and visits garden bird feeders.*

Although often seen in gardens, the diminutive white-naped Coal Tit is typically a bird of conifer trees, where it makes the most of its minute weight by searching the thinnest twigs for food. Active and fearless, it often joins up with other species of tits in autumn and winter, roaming through woodlands and gardens in large, loose, mixed flocks.

yellower cheek

black head

white nape patch

greyish back

black bib

white cheek

dark wings with two white bars

bright buff underside

VOICE *Call high, sweet* tseu, *thin* tsee, *bright* psuet; *song quick* wi-choo wi-choo wi-choo.
NESTING *Cup of moss and leaves in hole in tree or wall; 7–11 eggs; 1 brood; Apr–Jun.*
FEEDING *Takes tiny insects and spiders from foliage; also seeds and nuts; visits feeders.*
SIMILAR SPECIES *Marsh Tit, Willow Tit, Great Tit.*

Blue Tit

Parus caeruleus

VISITS GARDENS *to feed from nut baskets and other feeders. Lives in woods of all kinds, as well as parks, gardens, and bushy places.*

Colourful, tame, and noisy, the Blue Tit is mainly yellow and greenish as well as blue. It is a common visitor to bird feeders where its acrobatic skills make it a favourite garden bird. Its black-and-white face pattern is distinctive. A thin, dark central streak often shows on its yellow underside.

bright blue cap

white bars on blue wings

blue tail

♂

greenish cap

yellow below

less blue

♀

VOICE *Thin, quick* tsee-tsee-tsee, *scolding* churrrr; *song trilled* tsee-tsee-tsee-tsisisisisisi.
NESTING *Small cup of moss and hair in tree hole/nest box; 7–16 eggs; 1 brood; Apr–May.*
FEEDING *Mainly seeds, nuts, insects, and spiders; often visits garden feeders.*
SIMILAR SPECIES *Coal Tit, Great Tit, Goldcrest.*

Great Tit

Parus major

BREEDS AND *feeds in wide variety of mixed woodland, as well as parks and gardens. Often uses nest boxes.*

The bold, even aggressive Great Tit is one of the most familiar garden and woodland birds. Its calls can be confusing, but it is easily identified by the broad black stripe on its yellow breast. Less agile than the smaller tits, it feeds on the ground more often.

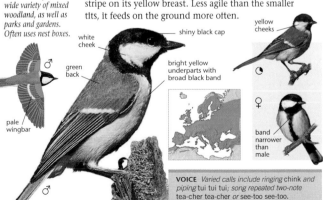

white cheek

shiny black cap

green back

♂

pale wingbar

bright yellow underparts with broad black band

♂

yellow cheeks

♀

band narrower than male

VOICE *Varied calls include ringing* chink *and piping* tui tui tui; *song repeated two-note* tea-cher tea-cher *or* see-too see-too.
NESTING *Cup of moss, leaves, and grass in tree hole; 5–11 eggs; 1 brood; Apr–May.*
FEEDING *Insects, seeds, nuts, especially tree seeds in autumn, winter; often visits feeders.*
SIMILAR SPECIES *Blue Tit, Coal Tit.*

Nuthatch

Sitta europaea

FORAGES HIGH *in trees and on the ground in deciduous and mixed woodland, parkland, and large gardens, all year round.*

Identified by its blue-grey and buff plumage and oddly top-heavy look, the Nuthatch is an agile climber that (unlike other birds) often descends trees head-first, as well as climbing upwards. It wedges nuts and seeds in bark so it can crack them open, with loud blows of its long, grey, chisel-like bill.

broad blue-grey wings

buff below, with rusty flanks

acrobatic pose

black stripe

dagger-like grey bill

strong feet for clinging to bark

short tail

VOICE *Loud, liquid whistles, pew pew pew, chwee chwee; fast ringing trills, loud chwit.*
NESTING *Typically plasters mud around old woodpecker hole lined with bark and leaves; 6–9 eggs; 1 brood; Apr–Jul.*
FEEDING *Variety of seeds, berries, and nuts, often wedged in bark for easy cracking.*
SIMILAR SPECIES *Rock Nuthatch (rare).*

Jay

Garrulus glandarius

Noisy but shy, the Jay often keeps to thick cover and beats a swift retreat if disturbed, flying off with a flash of its bold white rump. It has a curious habit of allowing ants to run over its plumage, probably to employ the ants' chemical defences against parasites.

BREEDS IN *woodland and parks, especially with oak trees, and visits gardens.*

moustache thick and black

pinkish grey body

barred blue wing panel

white patch on black wings

raised crest

"anting" posture

white rump

white under tail

black tail

VOICE *Nasal, mewing pee-oo, short bark; loud, harsh, cloth-tearing skairk!*
NESTING *Bulky stick nest, low in dense bush; 4–5 eggs; 1 brood; Apr–Jun.*
FEEDING *Eats mainly insects in summer, with some eggs and nestlings; stores acorns in autumn for use in winter.*
SIMILAR SPECIES *Hoopoe.*

Magpie

Pica pica

A handsome crow with boldly pied plumage and a long, tapered tail, the Magpie is unmistakable. In sunlight it has an iridescent sheen of blue, purple, and green. It has a reputation for wiping out songbirds, but research shows that its fondness for eating eggs and chicks has little overall effect on populations.

BREEDS ON *farmland with hedges, woodland edges, and urban parks. Visits gardens to find food.*

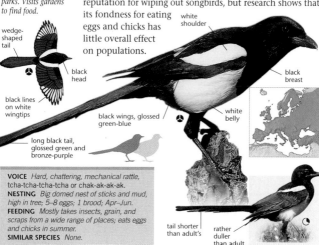

wedge-shaped tail

black head

black lines on white wingtips

black wings, glossed green-blue

long black tail, glossed green and bronze-purple

white shoulder

black breast

white belly

tail shorter than adult's

rather duller than adult

VOICE *Hard, chattering, mechanical rattle, tcha-tcha-tcha-tcha or chak-ak-ak-ak.*
NESTING *Big domed nest of sticks and mud, high in tree; 5–8 eggs; 1 brood; Apr–Jun.*
FEEDING *Mostly takes insects, grain, and scraps from a wide range of places; eats eggs and chicks in summer.*
SIMILAR SPECIES *None.*

Jackdaw

Corvus monedula

A small, short-billed crow with a black cap and a pale grey nape, the Jackdaw is a very sociable bird that often flies in flocks, performing spectacular aerobatics with much calling. It also feeds in mixed flocks with Rooks, when its compact shape becomes obvious.

LIVES AROUND *cliffs, quarries, old buildings, woods, farmland with mature trees, or towns and villages where there are old houses with chimneys.*

rounded wings

pale eyes

grey nape

black cap

grey-black body

short, thick bill

dark grey under-wings

VOICE *Noisy kyak or tjak! with squeaky, bright quality; some longer calls like chee-ar.*
NESTING *Pile of sticks lined with mud, moss, and hair, in hole in tree, cliff, or building, or in chimney; 4–6 eggs; 1 brood; Apr–Jul.*
FEEDING *Takes worms, seeds, and scraps from ground; also caterpillars and berries.*
SIMILAR SPECIES *Rook, Chough.*

TIP

Although similar to other black crows such as the Rook, the Jackdaw is distinctly smaller, with shorter legs and a shorter bill.

Rook

Corvus frugilegus

This intensely social crow is known for its loud cawing calls. Adult Rooks are distinguished by a bare, parchment-white face. It has a peaked, rather than flat-topped crown, and ragged thigh feathers create a "baggy trouser" effect.

BREEDS IN *treetop colonies, typically in farmland, parks, and villages or small towns with scattered tall trees for nesting.*

black bill base

bill thinner than Crow's

glossy black body

body deeper, less sleek than Carrion Crow's

looser feathers and slighter body than Crow

loose, ragged thigh feathers

rounded tail

wings more pointed than Carrion Crow's

narrow, rounded tail

VOICE *Raucous, but relaxed cawing, caaar, grah-gra-gra, plus higher, strangled notes.*
NESTING *Big nest of sticks lined with grass, moss, and leaves, in treetop colony; 3–6 eggs; 1 brood; Mar–Jun.*
FEEDING *Eats insects, seeds, grain, and roots from ground; also forages for roadkill.*
SIMILAR SPECIES *Carrion Crow, Jackdaw, Raven.*

Carrion Crow

Corvus corone

The all-black Carrion Crow is easy to confuse with other crows, particularly a juvenile Rook, but its head has a distinctly flatter crown and its body plumage is much tighter and neater-looking, with no "baggy trouser" effect. It is usually seen alone or in pairs, but may gather to feed and roost in flocks in autumn and winter, and often feeds alongside other crows.

LIVES IN *open areas, from farmland to city centres; also feeds on coasts and estuaries.*

flat-topped head

squarer wingtips than Rook

thick, arched bill

glossy black body

neat, tight body feathering

square tail

VOICE *Loud, harsh, grating caw, krra krra krra, metallic konk, korr, and similar calls.*
NESTING *Big stick nest, in tree, bush, on cliff or building; 4–6 eggs; 1 brood; Mar–Jul.*
FEEDING *Feeds on ground, taking all kinds of invertebrates, eggs, grain, and various scraps; usually in pairs but sometimes flocks.*
SIMILAR SPECIES *Rook, Raven, Jackdaw.*

Starling

Sturnus vulgaris

A common, active, noisy, sociable, but quarrelsome bird of urban and rural habitats, the Starling is instantly recognizable by its strong-legged walk and waddling run as it pokes and pries in the soil for insect grubs and seeds. Superficially black, its plumage is glossed with iridescent green and purple in summer, and spotted with buff in winter. Outside the breeding season it forms dense flocks that roost in trees, reedbeds, and on buildings, and swirl around the sky in perfectly co-ordinated aerobatic manoeuvres, particularly at dusk. These winter flocks can be so vast that they look like clouds of smoke at a distance, although declines in many areas have made such immense gatherings less common.

GATHERS IN *big winter flocks in forests, city centres, industrial sites, bridges, and piers. Breeds in woods, gardens, and towns.*

short, squarish tail

TIP

Starlings are skilled mimics and can even imitate noises such as telephones. A strange sound coming from an odd place often turns out to be a Starling.

sharp yellow bill

blue-grey bill base; pale pink on female

glossy black body with green and purple sheen

long, strong, red-brown legs

♂ ☘

silvery face with dark mask

body feathers tipped buff or whitish

feathers edged bright orange-buff

large spots near tail

dull head last to get adult colours

MOULTING

plain brown body

dark bill

VOICE *Loud, slightly grating* cheer, *musical, twangy, whistled* tswee-oo, *variety of clicks, gurgles, squawking notes; song fast mixture of rattles, trills, gurgles, and whistles, often with mimicry of other birds or sounds.*
NESTING *Loose, bulky nest of grass and stems, in tree hole, cavity in wall or building, or large nest box; 4–7 eggs, 1–2 broods; Apr–Jul.*
FEEDING *Forages for invertebrates, seeds, and berries on the ground, in small to large flocks; catches flying ants in mid-air.*
SIMILAR SPECIES *Spotless Starling, Blackbird.*

House Sparrow

Passer domesticus

LIVES IN *cities, towns, villages, farms, and on farmland; rarely found far from human habitation.*

This common, noisy sparrow is one of the most familiar small birds due to its habit of nesting in buildings. The male has a bold black bib and distinctive grey cap, but the female can be confused with a female finch. Although House Sparrow populations have declined, they are still widespread.

grey cap

big black bib

red-brown above, with dark streaks

unmarked grey below

whitish wingbar

greyish rump

♂

♂☼

pale stripe

plain plumage

♀

VOICE *Lively* chirrup, chilp, *as loud chorus from flock; song a simple series of chirps.*
NESTING *Untidy nest of grass and feathers in cavity; 3–7 eggs; 1–4 broods; Apr–Aug.*
FEEDING *Takes seeds, nuts, and berries, mainly from ground, plus insects for young.*
SIMILAR SPECIES *Spanish Sparrow, female Chaffinch.*

Chaffinch

Fringilla coelebs

BREEDS IN *coniferous and deciduous forests, woods, hedges, parks, and gardens.*

One of the least specialized of the finches, the Chaffinch is also one of the most successful and abundant. Unusually for finches, pairs breed in separate territories, proclaimed by males singing loudly from prominent perches. At other times they are social and often very tame.

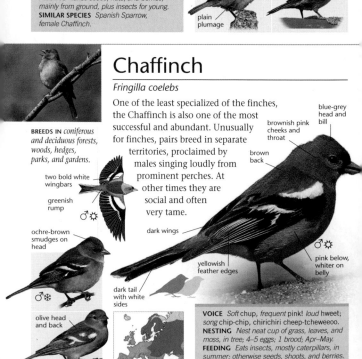

blue-grey head and bill

brownish pink cheeks and throat

brown back

two bold white wingbars

greenish rump

♂☼

ochre-brown smudges on head

dark wings

yellowish feather edges

pink below, whiter on belly

♂☼

dark tail with white sides

♂❄

olive head and back

♀

VOICE *Soft* chup, *frequent* pink! *loud* hweet; *song* chip-chip, chirichiri cheep-tcheweeoo.
NESTING *Nest neat cup of grass, leaves, and moss, in tree; 4–5 eggs; 1 brood; Apr–May.*
FEEDING *Eats insects, mostly caterpillars, in summer; otherwise seeds, shoots, and berries.*
SIMILAR SPECIES *Brambling, Bullfinch, female House Sparrow.*

Brambling

Fringilla montifringilla

Very like the Chaffinch, but with a white rump and a darker back, the Brambling is generally less common and very scarce in Europe in summer. In winter, Bramblings may gather in huge feeding flocks, especially in central Europe, but numbers fluctuate from year to year with the supply of beech-mast and other tree seeds.

FEEDS IN *farmland and parks, in winter, especially areas with beech, birch, and spruce; breeds in northern forests.*

white rump

big orange-buff upper wingbar

pale throat

"scaly" head

bright yellow-orange breast and shoulder

dark back

duller

white belly

dark spots on flanks

black head and back

♂☀

♀❄

♂❄

VOICE *Call hard chek, distinctive nasal tsweek; song repeated nasal, buzzing dzeeee.*
NESTING *Cup of lichen, bark, and stems, in tree or bush; 5–7 eggs; 1 brood; May–Jun.*
FEEDING *Eats insects in summer, seeds at other times; takes beech-mast from ground.*
SIMILAR SPECIES *Chaffinch, female House Sparrow.*

Goldfinch

Carduelis carduelis

Flocks of colourful Goldfinches feed on waste ground, farmyards, and field edges, picking soft, milky seeds from thistles, tall daisies, and similar plants with their pointed bills. They are agile feeders, often swinging head-down from seedheads, and have a distinctive dancing flight and tinkling calls.

bold black, red, and white head

FORAGES IN *weedy places with tall seed-bearing flowers such as thistles and teasels; also in alder and larch.*

tawny back

yellow on closed wing

tawny-chestnut patch

black wings

big yellow panels

pale underside

grey head

duller wings

VOICE *Call chattering, lilting skip-i-lip, rough tschair; song mix of call notes and liquid trills.*
NESTING *Neat nest of roots, grass, cobwebs in tree or bush; 5–6 eggs; 2 broods; May–Jul.*
FEEDING *Gathers soft, half-ripe seeds from thistles and similar plants, less often from ground; also eats seeds of alder and larch.*
SIMILAR SPECIES *Siskin, Greenfinch.*

TIP

At a distance the red face can be hard to see, but the yellow wing flashes and bouncy flight action usually make identification easy.

Greenfinch

Carduelis chloris

dark patch

Males are easy to identify by their green plumage with bright yellow flashes, and a "frowning" look; the duller females and juveniles are also stocky and stout-billed, but trickier to distinguish. In spring, males sing during circling, stiff-winged display flights.

FEEDS ON *sunflower seeds at garden feeders; breeds in open woods, hedges, large gardens.*

bright olive green

yellow stripe

♂ ☀

browner than adult

streaked all over

greyer above

duller than male

♂ ❄

♀

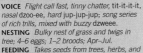

VOICE *Flight call fast, tinny chatter, tit-it-it-it, nasal dzoo-ee, hard jup-jup-jup; song series of rich trills, mixed with buzzy dzweee.*
NESTING *Bulky nest of grass and twigs in tree; 4–6 eggs; 1–2 broods; Apr–Jul.*
FEEDING *Takes seeds from trees, herbs, and ground; also berries and nuts.*
SIMILAR SPECIES *Citril Finch, Serin, Siskin.*

yellow patches on tail ♂

flashes of yellow on outer part of grey wings

Siskin

Carduelis spinus

A specialist at feeding on tree seeds, the neat, slender Siskin is particularly associated with conifers such as pines and spruces. It usually feeds high in the trees, displaying tit-like agility, and in spring the males often sing from treetops. In winter, Siskins forage in flocks, often with Redpolls.

VISITS GARDENS *for peanuts, but breeds in spruce and pine forest. More widespread in winter.*

black cap and chin

dark streaks on green back

yellow patch each side of black tail

♂

lime-green to yellowish breast

bold yellow wingbars

greyer head than male

like greyer female

♀

VOICE *Whistled tsy-zee; hoarse purr; song mixes calls with trills and hard twittering notes.*
NESTING *Tiny nest of twigs and stems, lined with down, high in tree; 4–5 eggs; 1–2 broods; May–Jul.*
FEEDING *Eats the seeds of pine, larch, alder, birch, and various other trees.*
SIMILAR SPECIES *Greenfinch, Redpoll, Serin.*

Bullfinch

Pyrrhula pyrrhula

Heavily-built, rather sluggish, and often hard to see as it feeds quietly in dense cover, the Bullfinch is unmistakable when it emerges into the open. The male is a striking sight, with his bold red, grey, and black plumage and bright white rump. Generally shy, its caution may be warranted, because it is often treated as a pest due to its taste for soft buds of fruit trees. It is seriously declining in some regions.

RAIDS FLOWERING *fruit trees in woodland, farmland with hedges, thickets, orchards, parks, and gardens.*

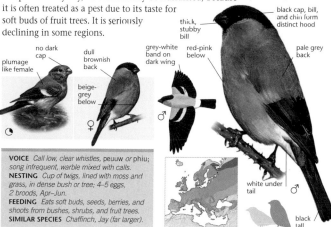

no dark cap

plumage like female

dull brownish back

beige-grey below

♀

thick, stubby bill

black cap, bill, and chin form distinct hood

grey-white band on dark wing

red-pink below

pale grey back

♂

white under tail

♂

black tail

VOICE Call low, clear whistles, peuuw or phiu; song infrequent, warble mixed with calls.
NESTING Cup of twigs, lined with moss and grass, in dense bush or tree; 4–5 eggs, 2 broods, Apr–Jun.
FEEDING Eats soft buds, seeds, berries, and shoots from bushes, shrubs, and fruit trees.
SIMILAR SPECIES Chaffinch, Jay (far larger).

Reed Bunting

Emberiza schoeniclus

Easy to find and identify in summer, male Reed Buntings sing monotonously from low perches among reeds and other wetland vegetation. In winter, when the males are far less striking, they are harder to recognize – especially when feeding on farmland or even in gardens.

LIVES IN *wet places with reeds, sedge, rushes; also gardens in winter.*

hint of pale collar

♀

cream and black streaks on back

long, notched tail

duller head pattern

♂❄

black head

white collar and moustache

rufous forewing

♂❄

bold white tail sides

brown back with black streaks

streaked, whitish underside

♂❄

pale red-brown legs

black tail with broad white sides

VOICE Call loud high tseeu, and high, thin, pure sweee, zi zi; song short, jangly phrase, srip srip srip sea-sea-sea stitip-itip-itipip.
NESTING Bulky nest of grass and sedge, on ground in cover; 4–5 eggs; 2 broods; Apr–Jun.
FEEDING Eats seeds, plus insects in summer.
SIMILAR SPECIES Female Chaffinch, Female Lapland Bunting, House Sparrow.

Bird gallery

The birds shown here are 40 of the most common garden species, grouped by size and family. Once you have identified a species, follow the cross-reference to its entry in the Bird Profiles section.

Goldcrest
8.5–9cm
p.97

Blackcap
13.5–15cm
p.96

♂

♀

Chiffchaff
10–11cm
p.96

Coal Tit
10–11.5cm
p.98

Marsh Tit
11.5–13cm
p.98

Wren
9–10cm
p.92

Blue Tit
11.5cm
p.99

Great Tit
14cm
p.99

Dunnock
13–14.5cm
p.92

Long-tailed Tit
14cm
p.97

Nuthatch
12–14.5cm
p.100

Goldfinch
12.5–13cm
p.105

House Sparrow
14–16cm
p.104
♂ ♀

Siskin
11–12.5cm
p.106
♂ ♀

Chaffinch
14.5cm
p.104
♂ ♀

Greenfinch
15cm
p.106
♂ ♀

Bullfinch
15cm
p.107
♀ ♂

Brambling
14.5cm
p.105
♂ ♀

»

Pied Wagtail
18cm
p.91
♀
♂

♂
♀
Reed Bunting
15cm
p.107

Starling
21cm
p.103

Mistle Thrush
26–29cm
p.94

Robin
12.5–14cm
p.93

Song Thrush
20–22cm
p.95

♂
Blackbird
24–25cm
p.93
♀

Redwing
19–23cm
p.95

Fieldfare
25cm
p.94

Great Spotted Woodpecker
22–23cm
p.90

♂

♀

Green Woodpecker
30–33cm
p.90

Collared Dove
31–33cm
p.89

Rock Dove
31–35cm
p.88

Woodpigeon
40–42cm
p.88

»

Jackdaw
33–34cm
p.101

Jay
34–35cm
p.100

Magpie
44–46cm
p.101

Rook
44–46cm
p.102

Carrion Crow
44–51cm
p.102

Sparrowhawk
28–40cm
p.87

♂

♀

Tawny Owl
37–39cm
p.89

Grey Heron
90–98cm
p.86

The Big Garden Birdwatch

Participate in the RSPB's popular Big Garden Birdwatch during the last weekend in January and make your garden birds part of the world's biggest survey of birds.

The Big Garden Birdwatch

After reading this book, you will hopefully become a lifelong fan of garden birds and devote some time to caring for them. Read on to learn all about the RSPB's Big Garden Birdwatch, the world's biggest survey of birds. Find out how to take part, and discover more about the RSPB and how you can give nature a home.

590,000 people took part in the 2013 Big Garden Birdwatch, counting a total of about 8 million birds

The RSPB's Big Garden Birdwatch takes place annually during the last weekend in January. From humble beginnings in the winter of 1978–79, when it was an activity for the Society's junior membership – then called the Young Ornithologists' Club – the basic principle remains the same to this day. To take part in the survey, you simply count the birds in your garden for an hour, then send in your results to the RSPB. The event has proved hugely popular in the three decades of its existence, and the number of participants has risen over the years – 590,000 people took part in the 2013 Big Garden Birdwatch.

The event takes place in winter, which is one of the best times to record garden birds because of the large numbers seeking food and shelter on our doorsteps.

Counting birds
Use the official Big Garden Birdwatch counting sheet to record your sightings over the hour.

How to take part

Taking part in the RSPB's Birdwatch is fun and easy to do. The more people that take part, the wider the geographical coverage area will be – creating a more accurate picture of how our garden birds are faring in the UK. All you need to do is observe the birds in your garden or local park for a short time during the last weekend in January. Simply spend an hour counting the birds, recording the highest number of each species seen in your garden (not flying over) at any one time. It's important you don't count all the birds you see because some birds will return to your garden many times in the hour. For example, if you see the same Blue Tit 10 times you have not counted 10 Blue Tits.

On the RSPB website you'll find a counting sheet, which you can download to help you keep track of how many birds you've seen. The sheet also provides images of the most common birds spotted in gardens and space to cross off how many of each species you have seen together. You don't need to send this sheet back to the RSPB – it is just to help you record your findings. You can submit your results online, using the survey form supplied. The results are published in March.

For more information, visit www.rspb.org.uk/birdwatch

What it tells us

During its 34-year history, the Birdwatch survey results have enabled the RSPB to keep track of, and compare, the fortunes of our most familiar and best-loved birds – those that share our parks and gardens.

Changing populations
The Birdwatch results have allowed the populations of the UK's garden birds to be measured over the survey's lifetime, revealing some substantial rises and falls.

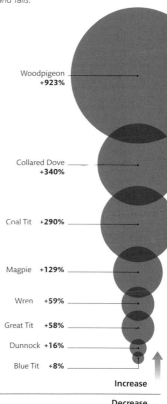

Woodpigeon **+923%**

Collared Dove **+340%**

Coal Tit **+290%**

Magpie **+129%**

Wren **+59%**

Great Tit **+58%**

Dunnock **+16%**

Blue Tit **+8%**

Increase

Decrease

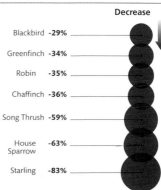

Blackbird **-29%**

Greenfinch **-34%**

Robin **-35%**

Chaffinch **-36%**

Song Thrush **-59%**

House Sparrow **-63%**

Starling **-83%**

TOP TEN BIRDS IN 2013

No two years are alike when it comes to the make-up of the Birdwatch top ten. This table shows the most common birds in the 2013 survey. (The figure for each bird is the average number of individuals per garden).

1	**House Sparrow**	3.7
2	**Blackbird**	2.9
3	**Blue Tit**	2.6
4	**Starling**	2.6
5	**Woodpigeon**	2.1
6	**Chaffinch**	1.9
7	**Great Tit**	1.4
8	**Goldfinch**	1.4
9	**Robin**	1.3
10	**Long-tailed Tit**	1.2

The increases, decreases, and "no-change" figures for each species are eagerly awaited every year from the results submitted by the hundreds of thousands of people taking part. With the same methodology used each January, it is possible to compare and contrast year on year and across the entire history of the Birdwatch.

Increases are positive news, but sadly, the Birdwatch has also revealed worrying declines for some of our most familiar birds; some species that were once very common are now a rarer sight. The annual publication of the Birdwatch results carries a serious conservation message too. Knowing certain birds are in trouble spurs nature lovers and wildlife gardeners across the UK to do their bit to help.

The Birdwatch has also revealed many species of birds adapting their behaviour and becoming garden regulars to take advantage of new foods and feeders. In the early years of the Birdwatch, Long-tailed Tits, Blackcaps, Chiffchaffs, and Great Spotted Woodpeckers were very unusual visitors to gardens.

Birds on the increase

Several species have started to become more frequent sights and sounds in UK gardens. In some cases, this reflects an increase in their total population that can be substantial. These increases add further weight to the important role that gardens play in conserving birds throughout the year.

The diagram on p.117 contrasts the fortunes of familiar birds and illustrates their percentage changes over the Birdwatch. The most spectacular increase has been

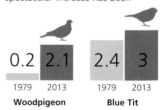

0.2	2.1	2.4	3
1979	2013	1979	2013
Woodpigeon		**Blue Tit**	

On the rise
The average number of Woodpigeons and Blue Tits per garden has increased, but the degree of change has been more significant in the Woodpigeon.

Gardens make up 4 per cent of the land area in the UK

Harsh winters
The weather is a key factor in bird behaviour, affecting the number of birds coming into gardens to feed. Jays prepare for winter by hoarding acorns.

shown by the Woodpigeon, up 923 per cent since 1979. This species can breed throughout the year, and has adapted to feed (albeit clumsily) from seed feeders and tables. These factors, combined with milder winters, help explain the increase. The average garden now has two Woodpigeons. Another species showing a marked increase is the Woodpigeon's smaller relative, the Collared Dove. This bird has colonized the whole of the UK since first arriving in the 1950s as part of its expansion across Europe from Asia. The Collared Dove is now found in most gardens.

Smaller birds can be hit hard by harsh winters, temporarily reducing populations, but overall Wrens and Great Tits show more than 50 per cent increases. Blue Tits show an 8 per cent increase, and the average number per garden is now three individuals. The easily overlooked Dunnock has shown a 16 per cent increase, despite its skulking nature and nondescript plumage, while the unmistakable and bold Magpie has seen a 129 per cent increase in its numbers over the period of the Birdwatch. This is a bird that has readily taken

to urban environments from a previously mainly rural existence.

Birds in decline

There have been some shocking declines in garden bird numbers over the duration of the Birdwatch. The House Sparrow and Starling are among the best known of all the UK's birds, but they have reduced,

Falling numbers
House Sparrows and Starlings have both experienced sharp declines over the course of the Big Garden Birdwatch.

10	3.7	15	2.6
1979	2013	1979	2013
House Sparrow		**Starling**	

Greater London lost

7 out of 10

of its **House Sparrows**

between **1994** and **2001**

respectively, from 10 to 4 and 15 to 3 individuals in gardens. Across the UK, this represents a severe population decline. The RSPB, along with a variety of partner conservation organizations, has identified these birds as needing urgent conservation action and they are the subject of research. Sadly, these birds have completely disappeared from many gardens. Lack of nesting sites (for example, in roof spaces) is a key factor for both.

Another shock is that perhaps our best-known bird, the Robin, has

suffered a 35 per cent decline. Song Thrushes have undergone a widely reported decline, noticeable in the now less-common sight of smashed snail shells next to "anvils" (stones) and a quieter dawn chorus.

Results such as these help the RSPB to prioritize its conservation work and take focused action for individual species. Garden owners have a crucial part to play for the Starling and House Sparrow. See the RSPB website for how you can help.

Unusual visitors

If you regularly watch your garden birds and familiarize yourself with the "locals", the array of species on offer will mean that you start to notice more unusual visitors. From Mealy Redpolls among the Lesser Redpolls on your nyjer feeder to Waxwings on berry bushes during the species' periodic "invasions"

Feeling the cold
Robins are badly affected by harsh winters. Many cannot survive a spell of freezing weather lasting longer than a week.

Black-throated Thrush
This Asian species has been recorded around 70 times in the UK, many in urban gardens including in the Birdwatch.

Little Egret
A rarity 20 years ago, this small heron is a common sight in wetlands. This increase has led to yearly Birdwatch records.

American Robin
With around 20 records in the UK, this bird is a rarity. Birdwatch participants found one in a garden in Bingley, Yorkshire, in 2007.

Common Rosefinch
This is a scarce spring and autumn migrant from eastern Europe, so a winter garden record on the Birdwatch was a surprise.

Little Bunting
This subtle, attractive Siberian straggler – a close relative of the Reed Bunting – has been found in a Birdwatch garden.

Yellow-browed Warbler
Following autumn influxes from Siberia, these tiny birds sometimes seek shelter in gardens if they remain here in winter.

from Scandinavia, everyone hopes for something unusual to report on the Birdwatch. Prepare your garden well and keep supplying food and water, and you may strike lucky – if not on the Birdwatch, definitely at some point during the year. Rare birds do not just occur on nature reserves or in remote parts of the UK, such as Shetland, the Isles of Scilly, and the tip of Cornwall. Gardens are such vital refuges for so many birds that unusual visitors frequently seek out the company of their nearest companions. For example, Rose-coloured Starlings from eastern Europe are found among flocks of our familiar Starling every year, and many vagrants from the US, including Baltimore Orioles, Dark-eyed Juncos, and White-throated Sparrows have welcomed an easy source of food provided in gardens.

Rarely spotted
With its orange crown and bright markings, the Firecrest is a distinctive, if seldom-seen, garden bird.

People taking part in the Big Garden Birdwatch have unearthed some truly rare birds. Some of them are spotlighted on p.121.

About the RSPB

The Royal Society for the Protection of Birds (RSPB) was founded in 1889 to combat the trade in wild birds' plumes. Since then, the number of issues the society tackles has increased enormously and its membership has grown to more than one million members. The RSPB could not undertake its vital work to help wild birds and other wildlife without its supporters and members. Such strength of support has enabled the RSPB to grow into Europe's biggest conservation charity.

Birds and their habitats are under more pressure than ever before. The RSPB is involved in a range of issues that affect birds and wildlife, such as conserving and restoring important areas for wildlife across the UK – including

managing more than 200 nature reserves, tackling wildlife crime, working with decision makers and landowners, and sharing expertise and knowledge to help young and old enjoy the natural world.

The RSPB helps wild birds both in the UK and, increasingly, abroad through a global conservation partnership called BirdLife International. Projects include helping to save the world's albatrosses from extinction and stopping illegal hunting of migratory birds in southern Europe.

You can support the RSPB in many ways, from becoming a member to making a donation and buying RSPB goods, including bird food, feeders, and nest boxes for your garden birds. Attend one of hundreds of RSPB events that take place all over the UK and join in the Society's Big Garden Birdwatch, and Giving Nature a Home wildlife gardening initiative. You can also volunteer with the RSPB or join a local group.

Red Kite
Once rare in the UK, this species has made an astonishing recovery.

For more information on the RSPB, its work and how to join, visit **www.rspb.org.uk**, telephone RSPB UK headquarters on 01767 680551, or write to The Lodge, Potton Road, Sandy, Bedfordshire SG19 2DL.

giving nature a home

Index

A

American Robin 121
anatomy 72–3
autumn 28–9

B

bacon rind 53
bathing 54–5
beaks 23, 73, 78
beech 69
berries 35–7, 38
Big Garden
    Birdwatch survey
    116–23
binoculars 7, 82
bird-baths 54
bird behaviour 84
bird cake 52
bird cherry 69
Birdlife International
    123
bird pudding 43
bird tables 46–7,
    50
Blackbird 5, 38, 85,
    93, 110, 117
    albino 84
    feathers 74–5
    food 38
    nest boxes 56
    singing 12
    young birds 26
Blackcap 30, 96,
    108
Black-headed Gull
    81
blackthorn 39
Black-throated
    Thrush 121
Blue Tit 99, 108,
    117, 118, 119
    courtship 15
    feeding 4, 22, 46–7
    nest boxes 56–8
nests 17
    singing 13
    territory 10–11
    wings 81
bones 72–3
borage 63
bramble 65
Brambling 5, 30,
    105, 109
bread 43
breeding
    courtship 14–15
    eggs 18
    nests 16–17
bugle 69
Bullfinch 24, 107,
    109
Bunting, Reed 107,
    110

C

cake, feeding birds
    53
Carrion Crow 102,
    112
cats 48, 50–1, 60
Chaffinch 20, 27, 30,
    104, 109, 117
chicks 18–19,
Chiffchaff 96, 108
clutch size 18
Coal Tit 98, 108,
    117
coconut 42, 45
Collared Dove 19,
    77, 79, 89, 111,
    117, 119
colours 74–5
common fumitory 63

Common Rosefinch
    121
compost bin 41
contour feathers 73
coppicing 68
cornflower 65
cotoneaster 39
counting birds 83
courtship 14–5, 84
cowslip 69
Crow, Carrion 102,
    112

D

Dove, Collared 19,
    77, 79, 89, 111,
    117, 119
Dunnock 77, 88, 92,
    108, 117, 119
    courtship 14
    feeding 47, 50

E

ears 73
eggs 18
eyes 73

F

feathers 73
    bathing 54–5
    colours and
        markings 74–5
    identifying 75
    insulation 30–1
    moulting 28
    preening 73, 75
    in spring 24
    in summer 26
feeders 46–51
    bird tables 46–51
    ground feeders 47,
    hanging feeders 48
    pole-mounted 48

siting 50–1
specialist feeders 49
feeding 22–3, 38–9, 84
  in autumn 28
  making food 52–3
  safety 26
  in spring 24
  in summer 26
  types of food 42–5
  in winter 30
feet 73
Fieldfare 5, 20, 30,
  38, 41, 94, 110
fighting 11
finches
  beaks 23, 78
  feeding 49
  flocks 10
  skulls 78
  in winter 34
Firecrest 85, 122
fledglings 19
flight 80–1
flight feathers 72
flocks 10, 28
Flycatcher 85
Flycatcher, Spotted
  56, 58, 78
food see feeding
foraging 23
foxglove 69
fruit 38–9, 53

G
garden
  country 68–9
  small 62–3
  suburban 66–7
  urban 64–5
globe thistle 63
Goldcrest 13, 28, 97,
  108
Goldfinch 28, 38, 41,

42, 47, 74, 105,
  109
Great Spotted
  Woodpecker 5,
  19, 25, 58, 82–7,
  90, 111
Great Tit 99, 108,
  117
Greenfinch 4, 6, 26,
  41, 54, 84, 106,
  109, 117
  nests 17
  plumage 74
  wings 80
Green Woodpecker
  11, 81, 90, 111
Grey Heron 86, 113
grooming 75
ground feeders 47
Gull, Black-headed
  81

H
habitat, garden 34–5
hanging feeders 48
hatching 18
hawthorn 39, 67
hazel 38, 69
hearing 73
hedges 36–7
  advantage of 37
  maintainance 37
  planting 37
Herb Robert 63
hoarding food 23
holly 67
honeysuckle 40, 67
House Martin 5, 20,
  24, 26, 36, 57,
  85
House Sparrow 5,
  26, 40, 77, 104,
  109, 117, 119

hygiene
  bird tables 47
  feeders 48
  nest boxes 57

I
ice plant 65
identifying birds 7,
  71–81
incubation, eggs
  18
insects and worms
  44
ivy 40, 66, 67

J
Jackdaw 81, 101,
  112
Jay 23, 79, 55, 75,
  100, 112, 119
John Downie crab
  apple 65

K
Kestrel 81
Kite, Red 123

L
lavender 63
lilac 63
Little bunting 121
Little Egret 121
Long-tailed Tit 97,
  108
Lesser Redpoll 38,
  42, 85

M
Magpie 79, 101,
  112, 117, 119
markings 75
Marsh Tit 98, 108
Martin, House 26,

36, 85
migration, 5, 20, 24
nest 36
nest boxes 57
mealworms 42, 44
dried 44
live 44
migration 20–1, 24, 30, 80
Mistle Thrush 94, 110
moulting 28

N

natural food 38–41
trees 38
shrubs 38
climbers 40
small plants 41
nest boxes 24
cleaning 28
making 58–9
types of 56–7
nests 16–17, 34
Nuthatch 5, 6, 23, 57, 100, 108
nuts 42–3
nyjer seed 49

O

Owl, Tawny 73, 89, 113
feathers 75
flight 81
nest boxes 57
senses 73
skulls 78
ox-eye daisy 65

P

pesticides 61
Pied Wagtail 24, 56, 91, 110
Pigeon 77, 81, 88
plumage see feathers
porridge oats 45
predators 24, 26, 46, 50
preening 73, 75
ponds 35
privet 67
purple loosestrife 69

R

raisin 45
record-keeping 7, 83
red campion 63
Red Kite 123
Redpoll, Lesser 38, 42, 85
Redpoll, Mealy 120
Redstart 85
red valerian 65
Redwing 5, 30, 38, 95, 110
Reed Bunting 107, 110
rice, feeding birds 45, 53
Robin 5, 42, 76, 93, 110, 117, 120
beak 79
feathers 31, 72–3
feeding 48, 53
fledglings 19
migration 20
nest boxes 56
plumage 74
singing 13
territory 10
Rock Dove 88, 111
Rook 81, 101, 112
Rose-coloured starling 122
rowan 67

RSPB 115–123
Big Garden Birdwatch survey116–23

S

seeds 41
hanging feeders 48
natural food 35–7
seed mixes 42–3
feeder mix 43
feeder mix extra 43
ground mix 43
no-mess sunflower 44
nyjer 44
sunflower hearts 44
sunflower, no-mess 44
sunflower, with shell 43
table mix 43
table mix extra 43
senses 73
shape, identifying birds 77
shelter 36–7
importance of 36
shrubs 38
singing 12–13
Siskin 5, 30, 38, 42, 75, 85, 106, 109
size, identifying birds 76–7
skeleton 72–3
skulls 78
song posts 10, 13
Song Thrush 85, 95, 110, 117, 120
Sparrow, House 5,

26, 40, 77, 104,
109, 117, 119
beaks 78
nest boxes 57–8
nesting 18
young birds 19
Sparrowhawk 50, 60,
76, 81, 87, 113
Spotted Flycatcher
56, 58, 78
spring 24–5
squirrels 47, 49
Starling 24, 36, 38,
85, 103, 110,
117, 119
beak 78
calls 13
feathers 75, 85
feeding 35, 48
flocks 10, 82
migration 20–1
nest boxes 58
wings 81
stinging nettle 65
suet
cake 44
balls 44
sprinkles 44
summer 26–7
sunflower 41, 65
Swallow 21, 23, 79,
84
sweet violet 67
Swift 82, 84
feeding 23
identifying 77
migration 5, 20, 24
nest boxes 57
wings 80–1

T

tails 79
Tawny Owl 57, 73,

75, 78, 81, 84,
89, 113
territorial disputes
84
territory 10–11
threats to birds 60–1
cats 60
pesticides 61
Sparrowhawk 60
thrushes 20, 34–5,
38, 77–8
Mistle 16–17, 94,
110
Song 12–13, 22,
47, 85, 95, 110,
117,120
thyme 63
tits 10, 77–8, 80
Coal 23, 28, 57–8,
98, 108, 117
Great 10–11, 46–7,
57–8, 99, 117,
119
Long-tailed 17, 79,
97 108
Marsh 98, 108
see also Blue Tit
trees 36

W

Wagtail, Pied 24, 56,
91, 110
warblers 78
watching birds 82–3
water 26, 30, 54–5
water plantain 67
water violet 67
Waxwings 38, 85
white water lily 69
wings
flight feathers 72
shape 80–1
winter 30–1

wisteria 40
woodpeckers 78, 81
Great Spotted 5,
19, 25, 58, 82–3,
90, 111
Green 11, 81, 90,
111
Woodpigeon 5, 19,
88, 111, 117, 118
Wren 92, 108, 117,
119
nest boxes 56
plumage 74
singing 13
tails 79
wings 80

Y

Yellow-browed
warbler 121

Acknowledgments

Dorling Kindersley would like to thank Ben Hoare for additional editing and proofreading, Nityanand Kumar for DTP assistance, Sakshi Saluja for compiling picture credits, Hilary Bird for indexing, and Tamlyn Calitz and Jaime Tenreiro for assistance with the project.

The publisher would like to thank the following for their kind permission to reproduce their photographs:

(Key: a-above; b-below/bottom; c-centre; l-left; r-right; t-top)

Alamy Images: Arco Images GmbH 60br; Juniors Bildarchiv 1; blickwinkel 15, 80; Les Borg 29; Andrew Darrington 25, 53; FLPA 40tr; Martin Fowler 93; Bob Gibbons 63cla; H. Mark Weidman Photography 39cl; Jeremy Inglis 121tl; INSADCO Photography 121br; Mike Lane 94; Renee Morris 2; Naturestock 84tl

Aquila Wildlife Images: Mike Wilkes 106tr

R.J. Chandler: 92bl

David Cottridge: 90cla

Corbis: Eric and David Hosking 93crb; David Cottridge: 90cla

DK Images: Kim Taylor 10, 13br, 16-17, 18t, 20, 22, 75t, 76b, 79

Dreamstime.com: Karin59 36b; Brian Kushner 121cl; Maasss 60bl; Mille19 38tr; Mike Nettleship 63tl; Psipc 121b; Dmytro Pylypenko 121cr; Olaf Speier 61bl; Verastuchelova 85c; Vasiliy Vishnevskiy 36tr; Whiskybottle 69bl; Steve Wilson 121tr; Zagrosti 119t

Fotolia: carmelo milluzzo 84tr; carmenrieb 38bl; Langer 41cl; lofik 67clb; Birute Vijeikiene 65clb

Paul Doherty: 101br

Göran Ekström: 101tl

FLPA: 97cb; Martin B Withers 89cr

Chris Gomersall Photography: 86br, 86crb, 88ca, 88clb, 89tl, 90cra, 91c, 92clb, 93cra, 93tr, 94crb, 95cra, 99tl, 100crb, 101ca, 102br, 102crb, 102tl, 102tr, 103bl, 103c, 104clb, 104cr, 104cra, 104tl, 106clb, 106fbr, 106tl

Mark Hamblin: 87fbl, 89br, 90br, 92crb, 94bl, 99fcra, 104fbl, 107br, 107cb, 107cla, 107cra, 107fcla

Chris Knights: 105crb, 105tl

Mike Lane: 91bl, 93cb, 93clb, 94ca, 94cra, 95ca, 96tr, 97br, 98ca, 105fcra, 107bl

Tim Loseby: 91clb

George McCarthy: 100cra

Alan Petty: 88bl

Photolibrary: OSF / Paulo de Oliveira 89clb

rspb-images.com: 4, 7tl, 42tr, 44tl, 45tr, 46bl, 47t, 48, 49br, 56t, 57tr, 67crb; Steve Austin 115; Nigel Blake 13tr; Richard Brooks 21, 90clb, 93br (immature), 103br; Laurie Campbell 12; Geoff Dore 70-71; Gerald Downey 79t; Bob Glover 14, 32-33, 55, 56b, 87tl, 103tl; Chris Gomersall 48bl; Danny Green 123tr; Mark Hamblin 87cr, 90crb, 95crb, 99br, 100clb, 107tr; Tony Hamblin 21b, 85br, 97tr; Andy Hay 11br; Robert Horne 98tr; Malcolm Hunt 97ca; David Kjaer 19, 87bl, 99cr, 118-119; Steve Knell 89bl; Chris Knights 91tr; Mike Lane 102cla, 106br; Gordon Langsbury 93cla; John Lawton Roberts 90tl, Mike McKavett 92tl; Philip Newman 95tr; Bill Paton 97crb, 101clb; Jodie Randall 114; Mike Read 54bl; David Tipling 8-9, 84b; Maurice Walker 98bc; Roger Wilmshurst 27

Roger Tidman: 86bl, 88br, 88tr, 89cra, 94cb, 96bc, 96br, 96ca, 96cra, 99ca, 99crb, 100tl, 103bc, 104br, 104c, 105br, 106fcla

Colin Varndell: 96crb, 98crb

Roger Wilmshurst: 101crb, 105cb

Steve Young: 91fclb, 92cla, 97cla, 101cra, 107crb

Jacket images: Front: Alamy Images: Colin Varndell t; **Dreamstime.com:** Iadamson c, Pretoperola b; **Spine: Alamy Images:** Colin Varndell b. **Back: rspb-images:** Laurie Campbell clb; Andy Ray br; Ray Kennedy bl,tl; Chris Knights clb.

All other images © Dorling Kindersley

For further information see:
www.dkimages.com